LEARN TO READ
THE EASY WAY

DEDICATION

For Euan, Lewis and Rose.

CONTENTS

INTRODUCTION

When you have a child, helping them learn to read is probably number one on your list of priorities during the early days of their education. We all know how important reading is for enjoyment and life skills, but it also impacts a child's confidence and the whole way they view education—whether it's at home or school. Reading is everything—and if it's an area you struggle with, it can have huge ramifications in every area of your life. But reading is also a joy. By reading, children and adults can escape to far-off places, have adventures, find out about people and places they never knew existed and open their minds to the past and future. Which is why it's so important to get it right the first time. The problem is that for some children, reading can be a chore, not something they enjoy or see the value of.

As a parent, if your child doesn't like reading, it can be both scary and frustrating, and not always something that you have much power to change once that mind-set has been created. We all know that if something isn't working, it's pretty senseless to keep going along the same path, which is why our approach to helping with reading is fresh, exciting and gives you as a parent the chance to spend quality time with your child not only in an educational way, but by sharing enjoyment and being creative, too. This book isn't about worksheets; our approach is tactile, hands on and active—using everyday materials that you either have at home or can buy extremely cheaply in your local dollar store. These activities also help promote other key skills, such as looking, listening, turn-taking, joining in, making choices, waiting and learning new vocabulary. As a qualified teacher and mother of three primary school–aged children myself, all of the activities have been "kid tested" and passed with flying colors!

This book is aimed at the four-through-six age range, although some of the earlier activities can be used with younger children from age two and a half onward. Later activities in the book—for example, in the Sentence Reading chapter (page 131)—can be used with older children, too. In fact, many of the activities in this book can be adapted for more experienced readers by just substituting more complex words that are suitable for your child's stage. You can use this book in lots of different ways. You can start at the beginning and work your way through in a sequential way to build up reading skills as you go and supplement what your child is learning at school, or you can pick and choose activities from any section, according to where your child has need. It's also worth going from chapter to chapter, trying a selection of word making, word games, sentence building and sight-reading activities to build up your child's reading skills, too. Some of the activities in the chapters are designed to be followed in the order written, and in other chapters, the activities can be done in any order—guidance is provided for this in the introduction to each chapter. Naturally, this book can also be used by educators who are keen to adopt a more play-based, hands-on creative approach to teaching reading skills. All are welcome.

So, what are we waiting for? Let's get making and start learning!

Heather McBean

GETTING READY TO READ

Before we begin, it's important to briefly introduce some of the terms and words used in this book that may be unfamiliar to you at this stage. There's nothing too complicated, and children usually enjoy using the more formal language to describe what they are learning.

Phonics is a way of learning to read through decoding certain symbols that also have sounds. Call it code breaking, if you will. Once you know the code, you can put those sounds together to make—and read—words.

Phonemes are the sounds that letters—or groups of letters—make. Sometimes, phonemes are made up of just one letter; sometimes, of groups of letters together.

Graphemes are the written symbols that represent the sounds, or the phonemes. This can be a single letter or a group of letters. There are often multiple graphemes for each phoneme—for example, the phoneme *ay* as in *play* can be written as *ai, a, a-e, ei* and *ey*, depending on the word you are writing.

Digraphs are graphemes with two letters—for example, *ea* or *oo*.

Split digraphs are digraphs that are split by a consonant—for example, in *l-a-k-e*, the *ae* sound is split by the *k* to give a long *a* sound. This is also called the "magic e" as the *e* at the end changes the sound of the other vowel in the word.

Trigraphs are graphemes with three letters—for example, *igh*.

Blending is when we put phonemes together to make a new word—for example, *c-a-t*.

Vowels are the letters *a, e, i, o* and *u* and sometimes *y* (at the end of words).

Consonants are any letters that are not vowels.

Consonant blends are when we put two consonants together and blend them to make one sound—for example, *br*.

Segmenting is when we break down a word to be able to write it according to the sounds we hear in that word.

Decodable/decoding refers to the process whereby we can read a word by sounding out each phoneme or letter sound. Some words cannot be decoded—for example, *said*.

Letter names are the traditional alphabet names that we give to letters—for example, we call the letter *b* "bee."

Letter sounds are the sounds each letter makes. When you say these, make them as short as possible—for example, an *h* sound should be like a short breath, not "huh."

Sight words are words that we see very regularly when we read. Some of them might be decodable, but some aren't and have to be learned by sight.

PHONEMES LIST

Here are the phonemes in the English language. Although the sounds can be taught in any order within each set, we recommend you follow the order of each list for ease of teaching and learning. When you do the activities, use the suggested set or replace it with the set your child is working on, checking off each sound as it is learned.

Set 1

_ s in sun

_ a in apple

_ t in top

_ p in pig

_ i in igloo

_ n in nest

_ m in map

_ d in dog

_ g in goat

_ o in odd

_ c in cat

_ k in kite

_ e in elephant

_ u in umbrella

_ r in rat

_ h in hat

_ b in bat

_ f in fan

_ l in lip

_ j in jam

_ v in van

_ w in wig

_ x in fox

_ y in yell

_ z in zip

_ qu in queen

Set 2

_ ff in puff

_ ll in sell

_ ss in kiss

_ zz in fuzz

_ ck in lock

A note about q

It is often easy to write out the 26 letters of the alphabet to help practice the different letter sounds—after all, the single letter phonemes are all alphabet letters; they just use the sounds instead of the names. The only exception to this, however, is the letter q. It is important to teach your child from the very beginning, that while q may have an alphabet name, it makes no sound when it is by itself. This is because, in the English language, q must always be put with its letter-buddy u to make a sound—qu, as in the word queen. Teaching and reinforcing this fundamental fact from the start will really help your child as they learn to read and, later, write.

Set 3

_ *ch* in *ch*in

_ *sh* in *sh*ip

_ *th* in *th*in and *th*is

_ *wh* in *wh*ip

_ *ng* in sa*ng*

_ *nk* in sa*nk*

Set 4

_ *ai* in r*ai*n

_ *ee* in f*ee*t

_ *igh* in n*igh*t

_ *oa* in b*oa*t

_ *oo* in b*oo*t

_ *ur* in h*ur*t

_ *ar* in f*ar*m

_ *or* in f*or*k

_ *oi* in *oi*l

_ *ow* in *ow*l

_ *oo* in c*oo*k

The following sets contain alternative spellings for each of the previously learned sounds, plus some new sounds and spelling patterns that exist outside these phonemes. The most common spellings for each sound are **bolded** and we recommend that you mainly focus on these, although less common spellings have also been listed for you.

Set 5

_ *ai*–**a-e, ay, eigh, a,** ei, ey, ea

_ *ee*–**e-e, e, ea, y,** ey, ie, i, ei

_ *igh*–**i-e, i, y, ie,** ye, y-e

_ *oa*–**o-e, o, oe, ow,** ou, ough

_ *oo*–**u-e, ue, u, ew,** ui, ou, ough, eu

Set 6

_ *ur*–**er, ir,** u-e, ar, or, ear

_ *ar*–or

_ *or*–oor, our, oar, ore

Set 7

_ *oi*–**oy**

_ *ow*–**ou**

_ *oo* (short sound)–**u**

_ *sh*–**ti, si, ci**

_ *zh*–**si**

Set 8

_ *aw* in j*aw* (plus alternative sounds **aul, wa, squa**)

_ *awl* as pronounced in b**al**d and w**all**

_ *awk* as pronounced in t**alk**

Set 9

_ *s* spelled *c* as in *c*ent

_ *j* spelled *g, ge* and *dge* as in *g*iant, *g*eneral and fu*dge*

_ *f* spelled *ph* as in *ph*onics

_ *k* spelled *ch* as in *ch*orus

_ *sh* spelled *ch* as in *ch*ef

Remember to go through each of the sounds suggested for each activity before starting.

When doing the activities, make sure that you hand print the letters and words as clearly as you can, to make it easy for your child to read.

LISTENING BOTTLES

Young children often find listening and paying attention quite tricky—which is understandable, considering how interesting the world is to them and how many new things they learn each day. But listening—specifically, listening for environmental sounds—is key to effective reading skills and needs to be practiced for children to be ready for learning to read. Making a listening bottle is a really fun way of introducing children to the concept of listening and joining in, in a tactile way.

Supplies

Recycled clear plastic bottles or containers with lids

Selection of objects to go inside each bottle, such as:

Lentils

Dried pasta

Uncooked rice

Buttons

Sticky tape (optional)

Tinfoil

How to

1. Place a handful of your choice of small objects inside each bottle (one type of object per bottle), making sure the bottle is never more than half full. It might be a good idea to seal the cap with a little sticky tape—just in case! It's important that the children see and feel the objects that are going inside each bottle, so they can match the sound during the learning. When you're done, wrap each bottle with tinfoil so your child can't see the contents, then rearrange the bottles a little on your work surface so they are in a different order.

2. Ask your child to shake each bottle, one at a time. Ask them what they hear, what it sounds like and which object they think might be inside and why. Then, change places—you shake, then see whether you can guess, too. Modeling this kind of behavior is great for encouraging your child to try new things.

Extension Ideas

Make a second set of bottles with the same objects inside and wrap them with tinfoil, then ask your child to match up the bottles! For instance, shake the bottle that the rice is in and ask them to identify the other bottle that also contains rice. For each matchup that they get right, they get a point.

Learning

During this activity, children are learning to listen carefully to different sounds and figure out how to differentiate between them. They will also learn that when the same kind of object is shaken in two different bottles, the bottles sound the same and therefore listeners can assume that they contain the same object. The same applies to sounds in words. The children are also learning about turn-taking, explaining what they think and why and using equipment safely.

PLAYDOUGH LETTER MAKING

Kids love playdough–fact! It's easy to make, feels good, makes lots of different things and is also wonderful for fine motor skills and getting those little fingers ready for writing, drawing and creating. Playdough is also great for reinforcing letter recognition–this one definitely feels more like play, but the learning elements are there in buckets! This is also a great activity to pack up and bring out when you get a spare moment, or if you are doing household tasks, it can keep a child busy.

For this activity, you can either make your own playdough or buy it from your local dollar store.

Supplies

2 tubs playdough

Child's rolling pin

Letter-shaped cutters (a complete alphabet; lowercase will work best)

Recommended sounds: any from Set 1 (page 12)

How to

1. Give your child their own ball of playdough, and have your own, too. Roll it out flat, using the rolling pin (great for fine motor skills!). Choose one letter-shaped cutter at a time, say the letter name, use the cutter to cut the letter from the playdough, then put it to one side.

2. Once all the letters are cut out, go through the letter cutouts, one at a time, challenging your child to say the letter sound and the letter name.

Extension Ideas

Gather the playdough back into a ball and take a small piece in your hand. Shape it to make one of the letters your child is familiar with (without using the cutters) and see if they can spot which letter it is.

Learning

Playdough is a tactile way of learning and combines fine motor skill development with sensory exploration. Children learn how to physically create letters using all their senses, and it's great for prewriting skills, too.

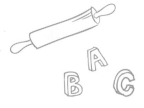

LETTER SOUP

Kids love cooking! And calling something "letter soup" is bound to get their attention!
This activity is one that is super easy to make and great for filling up time when you are preparing an evening meal—in a meaningful and fun way.

Supplies

Plastic letters (available at dollar stores) or alphabet pasta (dried)

Large pot

Wooden spoon

Small bowls

Recommended sounds: any from Set 1 (page 12)

How to

1. Give your child the letters and ask them to put them in the pot one at a time. If they already know their letter sounds, ask them to say the letter's sound (not name) before adding each to the pot. If they don't, ask them to show each letter to you; they then have to repeat the sound before adding the letter to the pot. Giving it a stir each time, of course!

2. Once all the letters are added to the "soup," ask your child to portion them into the bowls as "servings." Pointing to each letter, see whether your child can recall the letter sound (and name), then challenge them to think of a word that starts with that letter. If they are just at the start of their reading journey, restrict the number of letters you use (use the phonemes list on page 12) if you can, but use each one multiple times as it's all good practice.

Extension Ideas

See whether your child—with your support—can make short words from the letters in each bowl. If you used the pasta, it's also fun to cook it and, when it's cool, make a word, then eat it! As your child grows in confidence, introduce more and more letters to the "soup." Words you could make (depending on your child's stage) include at, a, as, it, sat, pat, tap, sap, sit, pit, tip, pip, sip.

Learning

During this activity, children get a chance to practice reading individual letters in a fun and hands-on way. Doing activities like this, where children can be independent and touch what they are doing, makes it more likely that they will remember the learning that takes place and apply it in the future. If using cooked pasta, eating the words afterward is fun, too, and helps the process of memorization.

MATCH THOSE LETTERS!

Letter-matching activities are a great way for children to start to look at the shape of letters and relate them to the sound the letter makes. This activity helps children sort and identify different letters using everyday household materials you would otherwise recycle.

Supplies

Marker

12 milk bottle caps (washed first)

Egg carton with 12 divots

Extension Ideas

Once your child is comfortable with matching up all the letters, introduce the concept of upper- and lowercase. Get new egg cartons and write the capital letters of the alphabet onto them, following the same idea, then ask your child to say each letter on the bottle caps and match it to its corresponding capital. You can also use the bottle caps to form short words, using your child's phonic knowledge to guide you.

How to

1. Using your marker, write twelve of the Set 1 letters (page 12) on the bottle caps (remember, instead of writing *q*, make sure you write *qu*). Write the letters in lowercase and make them all a consistent size, if you can. Use a bright color to make it more fun! Go through each of the letter sounds with your child.

2. Now, take your egg carton and, in a random order, write the same twelve letters on the base of each egg divot, again in lowercase.

3. Place your milk bottle caps all together in a pile. Ask your child to pick up one cap at a time and match it to the corresponding letter in the egg carton, saying the letter sound as they go. Once your child is confident with those twelve letters, use another egg carton and more bottle caps to work on the next twelve letters from Set 1, repeating until all the letters are learned.

Learning

This is a great activity for consolidating letter sounds—and building up gradually so that children don't become overwhelmed with all 26 letters at the same time. Matching up the letters helps children memorize the letter sounds, as well as start to connect the shape of the letter with the sound it makes—with a brief introduction to upper- and lowercase letters, too!

Rose

BENDY LETTERS

Challenge your child to start to think about spelling their name, and the other letters they know, by using pipe cleaners and bending them into the appropriate shape. Great for fine motor skills, but also works a treat for letter recognition and consolidation, too. You can also make some silly and funny shapes for added fun!

Supplies

Sheet of paper

Pen or pencil

Pipe cleaners

Recommended sounds: any from Set 1 (page 12)

How to

1. Write your child's name in large letters on the sheet of paper. Show your child their name and trace over it with your fingertips, encouraging them to do the same thing. Now, using their finger, have them practice writing their name in the air or on a flat surface, saying each letter's name as you go (unless the child's name can be spelled phonetically, in which case you can use the letter sounds—not many names can be!).

2. Next, take a pipe cleaner and show your child how to bend it to form the first letter of your child's name, saying the letter name as you do so. Place it down on your surface and continue, letter by letter, with the rest of the name. When you're done, ask your child whether there are any other words they think they can make. Again, write out the word on paper and practice first tracing the letters and writing the word in the air to get the shape right.

Extension Ideas

When you've made some letter shapes with the pipe cleaners, jumble them up and choosing one at a time, challenge your child to say the letter name and the letter sound. Then, try arranging them into new words.

Learning

Using this fun approach to tracing and forming letters, children will get a good feel for the physical shape of letters and words, as well as learning and reinforcing the letter names and sounds. This is a useful skill for reading as well as developing writing skills.

LETTER CRAFT CREATIONS

Making the association between upper- and lowercase letters is an important skill for children to learn. They might first start to notice that their name begins with an uppercase (or capital) letter, and sometimes children go on to write this same letter as uppercase every time they encounter it. For this reason, and many others, it's important to teach them the difference, including the times when it's appropriate to use lower- versus uppercase.

Supplies

Card stock

Marker

Scissors

Any craft supplies you have; e.g., crepe paper, stickers, glitter

Glue

Extension Ideas

Try cutting out the shape of the same lower- and uppercase letter and have your child decorate each one side by side. Do the same for the first letter of the name of each person in your family.

How to

1. Ask your child to pick out a letter of their choice—choosing the first letter of their name would probably be a good place to start. Show them how to draw the outline of this letter with a marker onto a piece of card stock so it almost fills the whole page. Explain that this is an uppercase letter, and show them some examples of the same letter in lowercase in a book, or just write it out.

2. Now, cut out the letter and ask your child to decorate it however they like, but they must choose a theme that starts with their letter. So, if their letter is a *C*, they must decorate it like a caterpillar; an *S*, like a snake; an *O*, like an orange and so on. Show your child how to trace their finger over the letter to get a feel for its shape.

Learning

By introducing the concept of upper- and lowercase letters in a fun way, children are more likely to remember how to read and use them in the future. Making mental associations between the letter shape and an object that begins with that letter makes it easier for children to recall their learning at the right moment.

MAKE-A-NAME WRISTBANDS

Children love making bracelets and wristbands, so why not combine that creativity with teaching your child how to read and recognize their own name? Name recognition is really important when starting at any childcare or school setting, mainly so your child will know where to put their things. But as it is also the first step on a journey to reading, why not do this in a superfun way?

Supplies

Paper

Felt-tip pens or colored pencils

Scissors

Glue or sticky tape

How to

1. Show your child how to write their name onto a piece of paper, but leave small gaps between each letter. Then, cut out each letter so it's in its own square and ask your child to decorate it. If your child's name is quite long, you might need to make these letters fairly small so they can fit on the wristband.

2. Now, it's time to make your wristband! Using the photo on page 28 as a guide, sketch out your own wristband's shape, then cut it out, cutting two slits to be able to attach the bracelet together. Ask your child to decorate it; then, to stick each letter square onto the wristband in the right order. Bend it around your child's wrist and attach the ends to form a ring. Point to each letter in turn, sounding each one out, then ask your child to do the same. If you need to make it more secure, feel free to add a little glue or tape.

3. Throughout the day, ask your child to keep looking at their wristband and spell out their name—it doesn't matter whether they say the letter sounds or letter names at this stage.

Extension Ideas

It's also pretty important for a child to learn how to spell and write their surname (last name), as well as their first name. Add an extra level of challenge in this activity by repeating the above activity but including a surname as well.

Learning

Having a child's name on their wrist all day will help them commit their name to memory, as it will be constantly in their line of vision. This will be really useful for helping them recognize their name on their possessions and to help them gain confidence for reading.

BUBBLE WRAP POP

Who can resist the temptation of popping Bubble Wrap? There's something really satisfying about it—and once you start popping, it's difficult to stop! This is a game that you can make as difficult or as easy as you like, according to your child's ability.

Supplies

Marker

Roll of Bubble Wrap that has large bubbles

Recommended sounds: any from Sets 1–4 (pages 12–13), depending on your child's stage

How to

1. Begin simply by writing a sound on each bubble—don't do it in alphabetical order; instead, be guided by sounds you know your child is already confident with (so they can practice and reinforce them) and sounds you know they need a little work with. When you're done, say one of the sounds and ask your child to pop the corresponding bubble. Continue until all the bubbles are popped.

2. Now, make it trickier! Using another sheet of Bubble Wrap, write some short words on each bubble, using letters that your child knows. Say each word and ask your child to pop the right bubble. Short words you could use are:

in, it, at, as, is, on

Learning

The challenge of searching for the correct letter or word means that children will have to listen carefully to the letter sound as they hear it spoken, matching it with the corresponding grapheme, and they will have to really focus and put some thought into what they're doing—which means they will learn more.

Extension Ideas

Take a new sheet of Bubble Wrap. Think of some short words, then write the sounds from those words on each bubble, say the word aloud and ask your child to make the word by popping the right letters—blending the word aloud as they go. Examples of words you could write are:

Set 1 words:

bat, dog, fan, peg, big, cat, mom, dad, box, van, quiz

Set 2 words:

sniff, fluff, yell, bill, kiss, pass, buzz, fizz, lock, duck

Set 3 words:

chin, chat, ship, fish, thin, this, whip, when, sang, ring, sank, think

Set 4 words:

rain, feet, night, boat, boot, hurt, farm, fork, oil, owl, cook

FISHY LETTERS

Let's go fishing! Fishing for sounds is a fantastic way of combining hand-eye coordination with letter recognition skills. There are a few ways you can make this game, so maybe include your child in its design—you never know what they might come up with.

Supplies

Paper

Felt-tip pens or colored pencils

Scissors

Paperclips

Wool or twine

Stick—a chopstick works fine

Small magnet—available from dollar stores

Glue dots

Large plastic bowl to put the fish in (optional)

Recommended sounds: any from Sets 1–4 (pages 12–13), depending on your child's stage

How to

1. Draw a series of fish shapes on your paper, then cut them out. On each fish, write a sound—include ones that you know your child knows, as well as sounds they may be just learning. Remember to include the letters from your child's name, as that can form part of the challenge.

2. On each fish, attach a paperclip near its head—feel free to ask your child to decorate each fish, too!

3. Then, prepare your rod: Wrap some wool around the top of your stick, tie it on with a knot, then attach a magnet to the end of the strand, using a glue dot. Put the fish in a large plastic bowl.

4. Now you're ready to start your game! Begin by asking your child to fish out specific sounds; they get a point for each one they get right. Then, see whether they can fish out sounds from short words—and their own name. You could even ask your child to challenge you to fish out some sounds. This way, they still have to look at, identify and read the letters on the fish, but they get to be the "teacher"!

Extension Ideas

If your child is ready, you can add an extra element of challenge by fishing out letters to make a short word, asking them to write it down and then reading what they have written.

Learning

This activity focuses children's attention on looking for and reading specific letters. They will have to discriminate between the letter or word they can see, and the letter or word they need, making reading compulsory to complete the challenge. So much fun!

BOTTLE CAP BINGO

This is a great activity for parents and kids who want to spend a bit more time on letter recognition and letter names—in a superfun way! This is also the sort of game that you can take along to restaurants or on vacation with you, as it packs up easily, too.

Supplies

Sheet of blank paper

Marker

Ruler

12 milk bottle caps (washed first)

Small bag—drawstring is best

Recommended sounds: any from Sets 1–4 (pages 12–13)

How to

1. On your sheet of paper, draw a grid with spaces for at least twelve letter sounds. In each space, write a different letter sound. Next, write a different letter sound on each bottle cap—making sure that you use the same letters as you have on your sheet. Put all the bottle caps into your little bag.

2. Go through all the letter sounds on your grid, asking your child to point to each one and repeat after you.

3. Now you're ready to start your game! Pick out a cap and show it to your child, asking them to say the letter name; if they get it right, they can place it on top of the corresponding letter sound on the grid. If they don't, it goes back into the bag to be picked out later when there are fewer letters left on their sheet (which also makes it easier to figure out where each goes). Give prizes for a line and a full house!

Extension Ideas

Replace letters with words! Write short words on the bottle tops and short words in the grid spaces. Remember that this time, your child will be using letter sounds, not names, to decode the words. You can also extend this game so that you each have a sheet, so you are competing against each other and taking turns, adding an extra element and also practicing turn-taking and waiting.

Learning

This activity is great for letter recognition skills and learning the letter names, as well as practicing blending and segmenting when using the extension idea. If you choose to both play at the same time, it is also great for encouraging waiting, anticipating and turn-taking.

ACE ACCORDION

Have you ever noticed how much kids love pop-up books and things that move? That's because they spur on children's natural curiosity about how the world works. These cute mini accordions play into that, and even if your child doesn't particularly like putting pencil to paper, we've thought of ways around that!

Supplies

Plain paper

Scissors

Ruler (optional)

Pencil (optional)

Coloring materials; e.g., colored pencils, felt-tip pens

Camera phone and printer (optional)

Recommended sounds: any that come at the start of a word

How to

1. Holding a sheet of paper in the landscape position, cut it into four equal strips going across, using a ruler and pencil if needed to draw a straight line. This is good cutting practice for your child, but be sure to supervise.

2. When you're done, fold each strip into an accordion shape that has four sections. You should now have four squares to draw or write on for each strip.

3. Lay out a strip so it is flat horizontally. On the rightmost square, write a letter using dots—start with something your child is familiar with to build confidence. On the next square, ask your child to draw something that starts with that letter, and then to continue drawing until they get to the last square on the right. Turn the accordion over, and on the rightmost square, you or your child should write the letter again; this acts as a front cover. When you're done, look back over your accordion together and ask your child to identify the initial letter sound, and then the objects they've drawn using that initial letter sound.

4. Repeat on the other strips for as many letters as you wish! These are great to keep out in your play area for your child to look back over and add to as they please.

Extension Ideas

If your child doesn't like to use pencils, or perhaps isn't ready, you can adapt this activity by using your camera phone and asking them to look for objects around the house that start with the chosen letter, take a photo, print it, then stick it in their accordion.

Each evening, go back over their accordions and practice each letter, pointing to the objects they've drawn.

Learning

Asking children to create something themselves and think about the objects they want to include helps create a sense of purpose. Reminding them of what they've created and practicing the letters will trigger the memory of what they created and why, and will aid their memory of what letter common objects start with—key for reading! Asking children to think of objects that start with your chosen letter allows them to think about the letter sound and assimilate it to objects in their environment.

LETTER SOUND TREASURE HUNT

This is a really cute game that can be done either in your home or outside in the yard. You can choose to make it as easy or as difficult as you like, according to your child's ability and age.

Supplies

Chalk (to play outdoors)

Large sheet of paper (to play indoors)

Plastic letters—you can buy these in either single-letter or digraph form (two letters together)

Recommended sounds: any from Sets 1–3 (pages 12–13)

How to

1. If you are doing the treasure hunt in the yard, draw out a grid with your chalk and in each square write a letter name. Your kids can help with this, too. If you are doing your hunt indoors, just use a large sheet of paper to do the same.

2. Now take your plastic letters and hide them high and low, far and wide! When you're done, ask your child to find them and then place them on the correct letter on the grid. When they get them all, they've won—and they'll probably want to hide them for you to have a turn, too. Remember to encourage your child to say the letter they have found before they lay it on the grid. They can say the letter name and the letter sound, or just the letter sound if identifying the name is too advanced.

Extension Ideas

If you want to, draw out 26 squares and put the letters in alphabetical order to reinforce or introduce alphabetical order. You could also write out words and ask your child to find the letters, then unscramble them to make the word.

Learning

Asking children to focus on the letters they've found and where they go on the grid really helps them focus on their learning. Asking them to differentiate between the letter sound and the letter name is also useful as a reading skill.

MAILBOX MATCHUP

Have you ever noticed how much children love playing with empty cardboard boxes? You buy them a new toy, and before you know it, they're ignoring the toy and turning the box into a car or house for their mini figures! Now you can capitalize on this by creating your very own mailbox to help your child match more lowercase and uppercase letters.

Supplies

Cardboard box

Craft knife (for adults only)

Paint (optional)

Scissors

Plain paper

Pen or pencil

Envelopes

Pretend mailbag (optional)

How to

1. Make your mailbox from your cardboard box, using your craft knife (do this part yourself) to cut a slit big enough to post envelopes through. You might want to make sure that there's also an opening to get your envelopes out at the end, too. You could always paint it if you want to be extra creative.

2. Cut your plain paper into small rectangles, then write out some lowercase letters (one per rectangle). Write the corresponding uppercase letters onto the front of each envelope. Together, go through each sound with your child, using the phonemes list (page 12) to help you with the sound.

3. Now it's time to play! Scatter the envelopes and rectangles on the floor and challenge your child to match up the envelopes and rectangles—for example, matching *a* with *A*. Once they have done so, ask your child to put each rectangle inside its corresponding envelope, then post them through the mailbox (this is great for fine motor skills, too).

4. When all the envelopes are posted, your child can pretend to be the mail carrier and retrieve the letters from the mailbox, putting them inside a pretend mail bag, if you have one. Then, ask your child to deliver the letters to you, and you can check them together to see whether they are right!

Extension Ideas

Extend this activity to include the whole of Set 1 and, to add an extra level of challenge, put the envelopes and rectangles face down to make it into a memory game, too, telling your child they can only turn one thing over at a time.

Learning

Once children have a good grasp of the letters, it's useful to introduce the idea of lower- and uppercase letters, as some can look surprisingly different from each other. Learning to identify and differentiate between lower- and uppercase letters is a useful skill for both reading and writing, and the start of understanding grammar.

WORD FAMILIES

Word families are a great way to introduce children to the concept that new words can be formed with relatively little phonics knowledge by blending letter sounds together. Even knowing just a few letter sounds can give children a large reading vocabulary—and word families are a great way of reinforcing this and introducing them to the idea that they can generalize their knowledge of phonics. They will also start to realize that words from the same family rhyme and have a predictable ending. This makes learning words in word families easier and gives children confidence in their reading ability. To get the most from this chapter, your child will need to be familiar with the letter sounds in Set 1 (page 12), but if they already know those sounds, then you can skip the previous chapter and start here.

In this chapter, different activities introduce and consolidate the concept of word families. Since the activities are focused around the same learning concept, it might make sense to use different word families in each activity to avoid repetition, but the activities can be done in any order. Enjoy!

Word Family Lists

ab	ad	am	an	ap
cab	bad	am	an	cap
dab	dad	clam	can	gap
lab	had	ham	fan	lap
nab	lad	jam	man	map
tab	mad	ram	pan	nap
	pad	yam	ran	rap
	sad		van	tap

at	ed	eg	en	et
at	bed	beg	den	bet
cat	fed	leg	hen	met
fat	led	peg	men	net
hat	red		pen	pet
mat	ted		ten	set
pat	wed			wet
				yet

id	ig	in	ip	it
bid	big	in	dip	it
did	dig	bin	hip	bit
hid	fig	din	lip	fit
kid	jig	fin	nip	hit
lid	pig	pin	pip	lit
rid	wig	tin	sip	pit
				sit

od	og	op	ot	ox
cod	bog	hop	cot	box
nod	dog	lop	got	fox
rod	fog	mop	hot	
	log	pop	jot	
		top	lot	
			pot	

ub	ug	um	un	ut
cub	bug	gum	bun	but
hub	dug	hum	fun	cut
rub	hug	rum	run	gut
sub	mug	sum	sun	hut
tub	rug			jut
	tug			nut

LIFT THE FLAP!

As anyone who has kids knows, children love anything that they can touch and experience, and if it has a little surprise underneath to engage their natural curiosity, so much the better! This activity is a real keepsake, and something that you can go back to time and time again.

Supplies

Card stock

Scissors

Marker

Colored paper stock

Glue stick

How to

1. Cut a rectangle from your card stock, laying it down in a landscape position. On the right-hand side of your rectangle, write one of the word endings from the word family lists on pages 44 and 45.

2. Next, cut your colored paper into squares that are approximately half the size of your rectangle. Using the word family lists, write the initial letter of the words for your chosen word ending. For example, if you have chosen word ending *id*, write the letters *b*, *d*, *h*, *k*, *l* and *r*. This is definitely something your child can join in doing.

3. Then, glue a thin strip along the left-hand side of each square. One by one, stick them down onto the left side of the rectangle, one on top of the other, so you have a series of flaps.

4. Now you're ready to go! Beginning at the far left, lift each flap and ask your child to read each word, showing them how to blend the letter sounds together. See whether they can start to remember each word before it comes—promoting anticipation. You take a turn, too, getting a few wrong and seeing whether they notice—if they do, then say thank you to them for teaching you and that it's not making a mistake, it's just learning—kids love that!

Extension Ideas

Ask your child whether they can think of other words they could make with each word ending—make up your own funny words, too!

Learning

In this activity, children will learn to anticipate the word that is coming, and that they know more than they think they know! Lifting up the flaps, one at a time, will also help children understand the idea of segmenting a word and saying each sound in turn before they blend them.

PLATE SPINNERS

Children love spinning the plate to "reveal" the next word, and before you know it, they've turned reading into a fun game! To do this task, it is useful if children are familiar with the majority of the Set 1 and 2 sounds from page 12, even if they can't blend them together yet to make new words. It also makes sense to use a different word family than you've covered in the previous activity.

Supplies

2 paper plates

Felt-tip pen

Ruler

Scissors

Thumbtack

Malleable material, such as reusable putty or playdough

Paper fastener

Extension Ideas

Are there any four-letter words that your child can think of that might be part of the same word family? Challenge them to make a new top and bottom plate with some four-letter words— for example, *gl-ad*.

Learning

During this activity, children are learning that some words can be formed easily through learning one word ending and changing the initial letter. They are also learning about the concept of rhyme and that words with the same ending make rhyming words.

How to

1. Get two paper plates and lay them facing up. Using the felt-tip pen and ruler, divide one of the plates into four, as if it is a pizza. This will be your top plate. Using scissors, cut out one of the quarters, then write a word family ending to the right of the missing quarters. For example, *um*.

2. Now take the other plate, and divide it into four in the same way. On each quarter, write a different initial letter that corresponds with the word ending. For example, *h, r, s* and *g*.

3. Create the spinner (this is also something to do yourself): Using your thumbtack while holding some malleable material below the plate to avoid pricking your finger, make a hole in the middle of your top plate. Repeat in the middle of the bottom plate. The holes should line up. Then, push your paper fastener through so the two plates are attached the right way up so you can read the letters on both of them.

4. Tell your child the sound of the two letters together on the bottom plate, and then separately, the letter sound on the top plate. Show them how to blend the sounds together to make a word.

5. Now spin your top plate around to form new words. Ask your child to apply their new learning to say each word at first together with you, and then independently.

WORD MACHINES

Every time you call something a machine, kids are instantly interested! These word machines use the concept of word families to create new words instantly by using existing letter sound knowledge. To take part in this activity, your child will need to know most of the Set 1 and 2 letter sounds—this is covered in Chapter 1 (page 12).

Supplies

Card stock—different colors if you have them

Scissors

Markers

Ruler

Paper knife (adults only)

How to

1. Holding a piece of card stock in a portrait direction, use your scissors to cut the stock vertically into four equal-sized strips (do this part yourself). On these strips, write a selection of the first letters from the words on the word family lists (pages 44–45), listing them vertically and leaving a reasonable space between each one.

2. Take a second piece of card stock, and this time cut across so you have four shorter strips. On each strip, using your paper knife (also do this part yourself), cut two parallel slits across the center. These have to be slightly wider than your longer strip so it can fit through the slits.

3. On your shorter strip, write the ending of the word family you have selected to the right of your parallel lines—for example, *ed*, *in* and *eg*.

4. Now you're ready to go! Simply insert your longer strip through the two cuts on the shorter strip and feed it through. Tell your child you are going to be using a word machine to make new words.

5. Tell them, or ask them to read, the ending of each word first, until they are secure with this. Then, go over the letters on the longer strip, one by one, reading them aloud together. When your child is ready, slide the strip down the word machine and ask them to read each word, one at a time, by blending the letters together.

Extension Ideas

Repeat for other word families—challenge your child to see how fast they can go! You could even try making words with some of the Set 3 or 4 sounds (page 13).

Learning

This activity is also great for teaching segmenting and blending for reading, as children have to first read the individual sounds and then blend them together to make the word.

BUILDING BLOCKS CHALLENGE

This is a must for building block fans and has the added dimension of actually creating something with bricks!
Sort the bricks into word families and see who can create the tallest tower!

Supplies

Sticky labels—any color or size that fits on the bricks (cut them if too big)

Marker

Large building blocks

How to

1. Using the word family lists from pages 44 and 45, write a selection of words on the sticky labels from the same word family, then stick them onto the sides of the bricks. Taking each brick one by one, practice reading each word with your child.

2. Now scatter the bricks around and ask your child to sort them into word families, pointing out the word ending on each brick. Your child can either gather them together or put them together to make a tower! When you're done, ask them to read out each word. As an additional challenge, you could play this as a race game to see who can make the biggest tower first!

Extension Ideas

Scatter the bricks again and ask your child to pick out a random selection. Read the words aloud and then put them in order to make a funny sentence! You can insert extra words as well, so your sentences make some sort of sense!

Learning

The act of putting the bricks together into a tower will help reinforce the spellings and sounds of the words in each word family. Playing this as a race game will also quicken children's reading speed as they go.

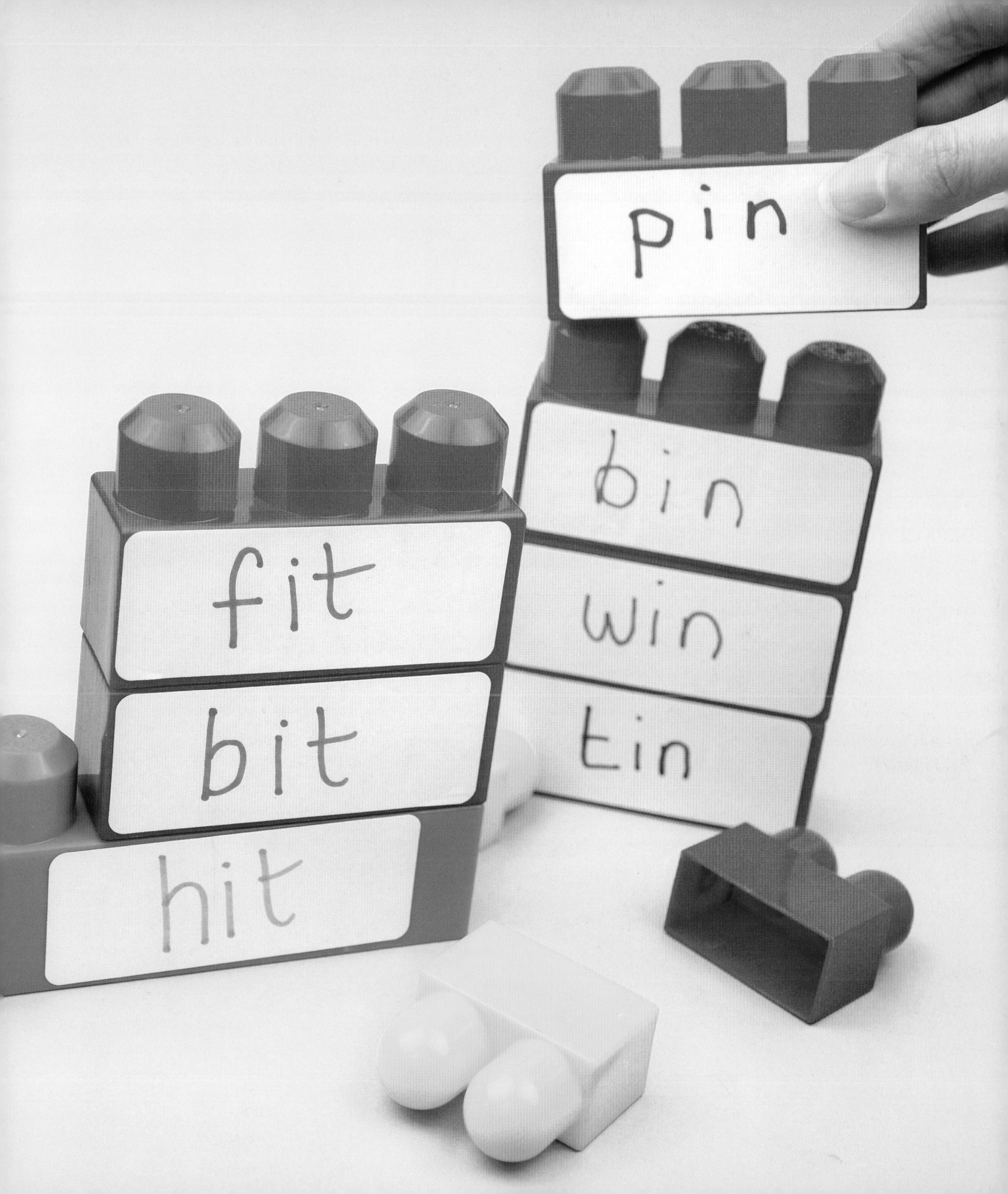
pin
bin
win
tin
fit
bit
hit

WORD DOMINOES

Dominoes is a really fun and motivating game that children love—and is especially enjoyable on rainy days and when you need some quiet time. It's also great for encouraging turn-taking and concentration skills—since, if you lose focus, you might lose the game!

Supplies

Craft sticks

Markers—different colors

How to

1. There are two ways you can make this game; both involve using words from our word family lists on pages 44 and 45.

2. The easiest way is to draw a line down the middle of a craft stick and, on one side, write a word from one word family. On the other side, write a word from a different word family.

3. Keep going until you have at least 30 sticks, but choose only three or four of the word families. Divide the sticks into two groups, then give one group to your child and keep the other for yourself. Start by laying down one stick and ask your child to lay a stick with the same word family, end to end, reading as you go. The first person to use up all their sticks wins!

Extension Ideas

The second way to make this game is to draw a line down the middle of the stick, and on the *right*-hand side, put an initial letter from one of the word families. On the *left*-hand side, put the word ending from one of the word families—for example, *ed, id* or *eg*. Continue until you have at least 30 sticks; try to use a combination of three or four of the word families. Then, play in the same way as described earlier, matching up the initial letter with the word ending to make the word. The first person to use up all their sticks wins!

Learning

So far, children engaged in these activities have only read words that are completed. By choosing which craft stick to use to complete a word themselves, this is a great way for them to gain confidence in forming—and reading—words independently, ready for writing!

WORD FAMILY CUPS

If your child is wriggly and doesn't like sitting down to concentrate, this is a great activity as it can be done anywhere. It also allows lots of twisting and turning and is a little less fine motor skills–focused than some of the previous activities.

Supplies

2 paper cups

Paper knife (adults only)

Paper (optional)

Glue (optional)

Marker

Extension Ideas

Consider making a word family cup with more complicated word families or sounds. You could use any of sounds from Sets 4–7 (page 13) to achieve this. Examples are:

-er (tiger, her, finger, letter . . .)

-ow (cow, how, now, allow . . .)

-oy (boy, toy, joy, enjoy . . .)

-ay (play, day, stay, spray . . .)

How to

1. From pages 44 and 45, choose one of the word families you haven't covered yet in the other activities. Very carefully, using a knife (do this part yourself), cut out a square window toward the middle of the cup. If your cups are patterned, you can attach some paper around your second cup to make it easier to write on.

2. Then, place the cup with the window on top of your second cup. Twist the cup around, and as it turns, regularly write in the first letters from the word family list you've chosen into each empty space that appears in the window. To the right of the window, write the word ending for your chosen word family.

3. Now it's time to play! Ask your child to twist the top cup around, reading each word by blending and seeing how the word ending stays the same and forms a new word with each new initial letter.

Learning

As your children progress through these word family games, they will have less and less need to decode the words and will start to recognize the shape and look of the letters. This is called sight-reading and is how more experienced readers are able to read quickly and effectively.

1A

1B

2

3

SPINNING WORD GENERATOR

This is a bit different than the rest of our word family activities. You can do this activity using word families or be a bit more adventurous and go maverick—making new words using different initial letters and different endings!

Supplies

2 cardboard tubes of slightly different diameters, such as from different brands of paper towels

Ruler

Scissors

Marker

How to

1. Using a ruler, cut your thinner tube in half crosswise, then cut your wider tube into thirds crosswise. Throw one of the thirds away, keeping two of them.

2. Holding one portion of the thinner tube horizontally, write the vowels *a*, *e*, *i*, *o* and *u* equidistant around the middle of the tube.

3. On the two remaining portions cut from the wider tube, also held horizontally, write a series of consonants all the way around, the same distance apart as the vowels, if you can. You can choose to use word families or use consonants from Sets 1–4 (pages 12–13), whatever you think is right for your child.

4. Attach the two consonant tube portions to either side of the vowels tube. The fit needs to be tight enough to stay on, but not so tight that they can't twist around. Now you have your generator! Spin each of the end tube portions one at a time and see which words you can form!

Extension Ideas

Try putting some of the digraphs or trigraphs from Sets 4–7 (page 13) into the middle section (avoid using *sh/zh* from Set 7) and see what words you can form now!

Learning

If you choose to use random consonants rather than word families, this is a good opportunity to talk about which letters form real words, and which letters don't. Nonsense words can still be read, however, and are a way to check children's decoding skills.

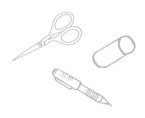

WORD EGG-STRAVAGANZA

Ever wondered what to do with leftover plastic eggs at Easter? This is a great way to reuse them in an educational way! Since the eggs are a little more fiddly to use than other activities in this chapter, they are also great for getting small fingers to grasp and twist with ease.

Supplies

5 plastic eggs that split into 2 halves

Marker

Extension Ideas

To extend this activity, you can put more than one word ending on the right side of the egg. If you do this, some of the initial letters might not make sense with the word endings, but that's okay! You can talk about which words are real and which are not. After a while, encourage your child to sight-read each word without trying to decode them—see how they do!

How to

1. Using the word family lists from pages 44 and 45, choose a word family you haven't looked at before and write the word ending on the right side of the egg (held horizontally). On the left side of the split, write the initial letter or letters in that word family. Repeat for the rest of your eggs until you've covered the word family you wanted to.

2. When you're done, twist the egg around to form each new word, asking your child to read each word aloud as you go, blending the sounds together. When they've got them all right, they can open the egg—so it might be nice to put a sticker or other treat inside as a reward!

Learning

By grouping word endings into families and seeing whether initial letters make sense with the word ending or not, this activity encourages children to start to discriminate between real and nonsense words. This is a great skill for writing, as it's important to try to figure out whether the word you've just written is a real one or not, as well as encouraging decoding skills, even when coming across unfamiliar words.

LETTER AND WORD GAMES

Now that your child has a good grasp of some of the most common letter sounds, it's time to apply their knowledge to something that won't even feel like learning—and that's where our games come in! In this next chapter, we will be focusing more on turn-taking games to help your child develop such key skills as anticipation, waiting for others to have their turn and waiting patiently— all important skills for life.

Before you start this chapter, you will need to go to the phoneme lists on pages 12 and 13 and introduce some new sounds if your child isn't already familiar with them. They should already be familiar with most of the sounds in Sets 1 and 2, but now need to be taught the sounds in Sets 3, 4 and 5. This will help your child complete the activities in this chapter. These games can be done in any order, or you can follow the suggested order. You can also reuse the ideas from each game and apply them to other future sounds that your child needs to work on.

OBB AND BOB SORTING GAME

The aim of this game is to read through a set of word cards one at a time and figure out whether the word is a real (Bob) or alien (Obb) word. Giving the nonsense words an "alien" tag means that children start to think clearly about which words do and don't make sense to them—and it also gives a chance for discussion around what makes a word real or not.

Supplies

Card stock or thick paper

Pencils, pens or felt-tip pens

Scissors

Glue

Ruler

2 containers—any will do; small trash cans (about 12" [30 cm] high) with free-swinging lids are perfect

Recommended sounds: any from Sets 1–4 (pages 12–13), depending on your child's stage

Extension Ideas

Challenge your child to come up with their own alien words based on the letters they already know. What is it about the words that makes them alien? What is their favorite alien word and why?

When your child is confident at reading sounds from Sets 1 through 4, start to introduce new sounds from Set 5 and onward (page 13) using new made-up and real words.

How to

1. Together, on card stock or paper, make some fun faces to glue on each of your containers—you can make them as crazy and interesting as you like. Be really creative! Keep in mind that one of the containers will be holding "alien" words—though, don't let that hold you back!

2. Create a name label for each of the containers—one is to be called Obb, and the other, Bob. Of course, you can make up your own names instead! Assign one of you as Obb, and the other as Bob.

3. Holding a sheet of card stock in a portrait position, cut across into five equal-sized strips (do this part yourself)—these will be your word cards.

4. Using the following word lists, or make up your own words, write one word on each strip—you can do this together if your child wants to, or on your own.

glog, chum, blot, tay, blard, kick, greet, sloam, disp, reef, dust, zued, murbs, short, parks

5. Ask your child to gather the word cards together and put them, face down, in a pile.

6. Picking up one card at a time, read the word together and decide whether it is a real (Bob) or alien (Obb) word. If it's a real word, place it in the Bob container; if it's an alien word, put it in the Obb container.

7. At the end of the game, look through each container to see which has the most cards. Whichever has the most wins!

Learning

Using the alien words means that children won't be able to sight-read the words and will definitely have to decode them—giving you a chance to figure out which sounds they might need more work on.

WORD TREASURE HUNT

This game has a different spin than our Letter Sound Treasure Hunt on page 38. To play this game, it probably helps to identify a mix of words that your child already recognizes, combined with a few they are having a harder time with. You can also mix in some household objects as well, to introduce something new.

Supplies

Ruler

Sheet of paper

Marker

Sticky notes

How to

1. Using a ruler, divide your sheet of paper into a three-by-three grid and on each section of the grid, write one word, such as door, cup, window, hat, mat, coat, table, chair and bed. Write the same words on your sticky notes, one per note, and on additional sticky notes, write some extra words that are not on your grid. When you're done, hide the sticky notes around your house in various places. If you're choosing to use object words as well, place those sticky notes on the corresponding object.

2. Now, challenge your child to find the sticky notes, taking the grid with them to look for each one. Ask them to read each word on the sticky note, and if it has a corresponding word on the chart, they should stick the note on top of that word. When they've completed the hunt, see whether they can find and read the extra words, too.

Extension Ideas

Try only writing the first letter of each word on your grid, with lines for each missing letter so your child knows what they're looking for. Ask them to find the object then write the rest of the word on the grid themselves.

Learning

During this game, children will start to associate words with actual objects, as well as consolidate the decodable words they already know and practice sight-reading. With reading, it's about giving children as many opportunities as possible in lots of different ways to encourage and motivate them. After all, reading is all around us; we just need to show children where to look for it.

door

hat   cup   door

chair   bed   mat

coat

window   table

SORTING BASKET

By now your child—and you—have probably picked up on the fact that some letters—and groups of letters—sound the same, but actually have a completely different spelling (see Set 5 and onward on page 13). This game gives children the chance to start to differentiate between these words and pick out the spellings and sounds for each word. Use our word card suggestions or come up with your own according to what your child is working on right now. You will need to show your child the sounds in Set 5 before starting this activity.

Supplies

3 containers—for example, pencil pots or bowls

Blank cards

Marker

Glue or sticky tape (optional)

Extension Ideas

Once your child has got the hang of the game and a feel for each word, change it slightly. Instead of them picking the card up, you pick it up and read the word to them. Ask them to point to which container the word should go into without looking at the word. Look at the word together to see whether they're right.

How to

1. First, label your containers. Make cards for the sounds *ai*, *ay* and *a-e* (or choose other sounds from Set 5) and place or stick them on each container.

2. Then, create word cards from the following lists:

ai	ay	a-e
Rain	Spray	Spade
Train	Play	Taste
Plain	Tray	Made
Snail	Day	Shade
Wait	Away	Safe
Fail	May	Hate

3. Put all the word cards, face down, in a pile. Turning over one at a time, read the word and choose which container to "feed" with the card according to the spelling of each word.

Learning

This game helps consolidate the idea that some letters and groups of letters have the same sound, but are spelled and look different from one another. The only way for children to learn the difference between the words is to practice, practice, practice!

"READ A WORD" COOTIE CATCHERS

Cootie catchers have long been a favorite among children—some people call them fortune tellers or chatterboxes—and are a great keepsake to have around and reuse. In this activity, you can make cootie catchers using words that your child is currently learning, or use the words we suggest—it's up to you! Again, review the sounds in Set 5 (page 13) before starting; we have included the most common ones here.

ee/ea/y: sheet, street, teeth, flea, treat, meal, happy, sunny, lucky

igh/ie/y: light, bright, night, tie, pie, fries, cry, dry

oa/ow/o-e: boat, coast, soap, bow, window, row, bone, cone, rope

oo/ue/ew: food, mood, smooth, clue, blue, true, flew, grew, threw

Remember to go through each sound before you start the activity.

Supplies

Plain paper

Scissors

Marker

How to

1. Fold your paper to make a square, cutting away the excess. Fold all four corners in, then turn over and repeat. Turn over again and fold all the corners into the center one last time. Now, unfold your cootie catcher so it's flat again, but has all the folds in place.

2. Next, it's time to write your letters! It's really important that you write them in the same direction as you can see in the photographs on page 71, as otherwise the cootie catcher won't work properly.

3. Finally, refold your cootie catcher so it's back to its original structure—and you're ready to go!

4. Holding the cootie catcher with your fingers, slowly open it up and challenge your child to read the word by looking at each letter, then open the cootie catcher to check that they're right! Continue until you've read each word. Then, swap places—your turn!

Extension Ideas

There are lots of ways to extend this activity to make it more challenging. First of all, you can ask your child to write on their own words—use trial and error to see what works. Experiment with longer words—what's the longest word they can create and read?

Learning

In this activity, children will learn how to read words that use different letters to make the same sounds. Use it for really challenging words that they are struggling to recognize—you'll soon see a big difference in their reading skills.

WORD MAKING

Now that your child has mastered a fair number of letter sounds and even words, what's next? Applying their new learning and making their own words, of course! Children are naturally creative and curious, so why not utilize this innate ability when it comes to reading? In this chapter, we've included lots of creative, easy and useful ideas for encouraging children to start to make their own words from their prior learning. By doing this, and with plenty of repetition, they will gain confidence and easily recognize these—and other— words in books and the world around them. And have fun with Mom, Dad, grandparents or caregivers in the meantime!

Before you start, go through the remaining sets from the phoneme list at the start of this book, from Set 5 onward (page 13). You can also review the previous sets, too, if your child needs a little reminder. It probably makes sense to do these activities in the order they are shown, so that your child can build up reading knowledge as they go.

BOTTLE CAP WORDS

Bottle caps are such a great resource to have when it comes to children's crafts and games, and in this activity, you can use bottle caps to encourage children to read and spell new words in a way that will be easy for them to remember. Here, we are going to focus on the long vowel sounds *ea*, *ai*, *ay* and *ee* from Set 5 (page 13), but feel free to use the words and sounds that are right for your child.

Supplies

About 20 bottle caps (washed first)

Marker

How to

1. On four of your bottle caps, use your marker to write the vowel sounds *ea*, *ai*, *ay* and *ee*.

2. Select some words from the following word lists.

> **ea**—eat, pea, seal, heat
>
> **ai**—snail, tail, paint, train
>
> **ay**—play, say, spray, day
>
> **ee**—bee, queen, cheek, feet

3. On the rest of your bottle caps, write on the other letters—for example, *e*, *sn*, *tr*, *pl*, *qu*, *ch*, *spr*, *n*, *d*, *b*, *c*, *h*, *l*, *s* and *t* (those that have a blended sound—e.g., *ch*—should be written together on one cap).

4. Show your child the vowel sounds and practice saying them—they should sound quite long (if you're not sure, try saying the words from the list).

5. Now, ask your child to use the bottle caps to make words that contain each long vowel sound. If they're stuck, have out just the letters needed to make the words containing that particular sound. If they're more confident, have out all the letters and vowel sounds at the same time.

Extension Ideas

Practice listening skills by saying each word to your child and asking them to draw what it looks like on a piece of paper (e.g., draw a picture of a bee). When they've done each one, ask them to use the bottle caps to make the word that goes with each picture.

Learning

Bottle caps are great for making games and activities for all areas of phonics, but showing these long vowel sounds on one cap will bring an awareness that this should be read as one sound, even though it's two letters. You can repeat this activity for other long vowel sounds *igh*, *oa*, *ey* and *ow* (or any others from Set 5 on page 13).

BUILD-A-WORD BLOCKS

Building blocks are lots of fun for little fingers and are developmentally appropriate for young children, as well as being a really familiar toy. Combine blocks with reading in this fun activity and give children the opportunity to make meaning from their creations!

Supplies

Sticky labels

Marker

Larger-style building blocks of various sizes

Extension Ideas

See whether your child can create their own words using the single building blocks. Another idea is to take the label off the larger block, mix the letters around and see whether your child can put them back in the right order.

How to

1. Choose either some words that your child is currently working on, or words using sounds from Set 5 (page 13). Here is a suggested word list.

clay	goes	blue	bird	pour
race	blow	clue	germ	door
boat	flow	grew	fern	more

Choosing one of the larger building blocks with space for four single blocks to put in a row on top, write one of the words you've chosen on a sticky label and stick it on, spaced out so that there is one letter per single block space. Now take the single blocks, and write the same letters, one per block, on sticky labels (you may need to cut them down). Repeat for the other words you've chosen.

2. Next, place all your blocks in a box or container, jumbling them up—and now it's time to play!

3. Challenge your child to choose the four-space building blocks (with a complete word on them) and find the corresponding letters to complete the word. Repeat until all the blocks are used up. Read out the words and see whether your child can figure out which are decodable and which cannot be decoded.

Learning

Playing with blocks is wonderful for fine motor skills, and the size of the large building blocks makes them easy for little fingers to manipulate. The physical activity that goes along with creating these words is really useful for helping children remember what they've learned. They do say you have to do something several times to learn it!

LOOPY WORDS

Children love playing with their food, don't they? So, how about combining the fun of that with making new words? If your child is working on words that contain an *oo* sound this is perfect, and even if they're not, this is a great way of introducing that sound.

Supplies

Sheet of paper

Marker

Loop-shaped cereal

How to

1. Using this list of *oo* words, write the letters out on a sheet of paper, but leave out the *oo* part of each word. Make sure you leave enough space to insert the pieces of cereal.

roof, food, moon, tools, smoothie, wood, cook, pool, book

2. Using the loop-shaped cereal, ask your child to complete each word. Point out that *oo* can have more than one sound. In this list, some of the words have a definite *oo* sound, whereas in some, the *oo* sounds more like *u*. This will of course differ slightly, depending on your accent.

3. When your child has read each word correctly, they can eat the loops from that word!

Extension Ideas

Challenge your child to use different-colored cereal loops according to the sound of *oo*. That is, if it sounds more like *u*, use another color than if it sounds like *oo*. Fun!

Learning

Children need to learn that some sounds may look the same, but they can sound quite different—it just depends on the word. The only way to figure it out is through lots of practice and learning what "sounds" right to them. Once they can do this, you know you've got a real reader on your hands!

PEBBLE PHONICS

Has the rock-painting craze hit your town yet? All over the world, kids are painting and then hiding rocks to help spread love and kindness, so why not join in the fun? This activity can be used again and again, and is a great way to take reading and learning outdoors, too.

Supplies

At least 10 clean pebbles, from your yard or a garden supply store

Markers

Nail polish—clear top coat (optional)

Extension Ideas

Together make a series of words with the pebbles to make a whole sentence. What happens if you rearrange some of the words—does the sentence still make sense?

Learning

In this activity, your child gets to use their fine motor skills to create words they already know, and maybe some they don't. The pebbles serve as a visual reminder of words they've already learned—why not make more pebbles every time your child learns a new word?

How to

1. You can either choose to use words that your child is working on right now, or if you are following this book in order, you can use these words. They've been split up for you so that, if you want to, you can write one sound per pebble, or else write only one letter per pebble.

earn—ear-n	**louder**—l-ou-d-er
pearl—p-ear-l	**ground**—g-r-ou-n-d
bird—b-ir-d	**about**—a-b-ou-t
third—th-ir-d	**around**—a-r-ou-n-d
dollar—d-o-ll-ar	**plum**—p-l-u-m
warm—wa-r-m	**muck**—m-u-ck
door—d-oor	**under**—u-n-d-er
floor—f-l-oor	**unlock**—u-n-l-o-ck
shore—sh-ore	**special**—s-p-e-ci-a-l
pour—p-our	**social**—s-o-ci-a-l
enjoy—en-j-oy	**casual**—c-a-s-u-a-l
loyal—l-oy-a-l	**vision**—v-i-si-o-n

2. If the pebbles are going to be kept outside, use a top coat of clear nail polish to seal them.

3. When you've created a range of pebbles, now it's time to make your words!

4. Ask your child to put the right pebbles together to make words, then blend the sounds together to read them.

Extension Ideas

Repeat by using sounds from Set 9 (page 13), including the following words:

cent—c-e-n-t

Cinderella—C-i-n-d-er-e-ll-a

center—c-e-n-t-er

face—f-a-c-e (split digraph)

circle—c-ir-c-le

giant—g-i-a-n-t

giraffe—g-i-r-a-ffe

general—g-e-n-er-a-l

wage—w-a-ge

sage—s-a-ge

judge—j-u-dge

fudge—f-u-dge

photograph—ph-o-t-o-g-r-a-ph

phonics—ph-o-n-i-c-s

alphabet—a-l-ph-a-b-e-t

elephant—e-l-e-ph-a-n-t

chorus—ch-or-us

chord—ch-or-d

Christmas—Ch-r-i-s-t-m-a-s

chemist—ch-e-m-i-s-t

chef—ch-e-f

brochure—b-r-o-ch-ure

charade—ch-a-r-a-d-e (split digraph)

chevron—ch-e-v-r-o-n

PING-PONG WORDS

Ping-Pong balls are the best! Cheap, light, bouncy . . . what's not to like? Combine them with egg cartons and you've got ready-made fun! This is a great activity that can be kept all together inside the egg carton and played with whenever you have a free moment.

Supplies

Marker

6 Ping-Pong balls (or more if you have them)

Piece of paper

Egg carton with at least 6 divots

How to

You can either use the words your child is currently working on, or the following words from the sounds in Set 8 on page 13.

s-aw	wa-s
d-r-aw	wa-tch
c-l-aw	wa-sp
h-au-l	sq-ua-sh
m-au-l	sq-ua-d
wa-sh	sh-awl
	c-r-awl

Learning

By rearranging the letters and putting them in the right order, children are learning that words follow certain sequences, and in fact, many words come from root words that help us figure out lots of other words. Very useful for future reading and learning.

1. Use your marker to spell out a word on your Ping-Pong balls, one letter per ball (or put one sound on each ball). Write down the same words on the paper as a list and show them to your child, reading each word together.

2. For each word, put the balls in your egg carton, but mix them up. Then, ask your child to open the carton and rearrange the balls to be in the right order to form the word. When they're done, read the word together by blending the sounds, then repeat the game for other words. This is so much fun!

CLOTHESPIN PHONICS

This cute game teaches children about consonant blends at the start of words. Use fine motor skills by getting those little fingers moving, pinching the clothespins to open them and using hand-eye coordination to put them in the right place. Encourage your children to blend the two initial letter sounds together as they read, rather than reading them as two separate sounds.

Supplies

Card stock

Scissors

Marker

Around 20 spring-style wooden clothespins

Tape (optional)

String (optional)

How to

1. Cut your card stock into rectangles or any shape you can write a word onto.

2. Write a selection of the following words onto the card stock rectangles. Alternatively, use words your child is currently working on.

club, drum, flan, from, glow, brag, grass, blab, plane, pram, scoop, skin, slip, smell, snail, spell

Leave a reasonable amount of space between each letter, so you have room to attach your clothespins. Read through the word cards with your child, concentrating on the sound at the start of each word.

3. If you want to, you can attach a string to the back of your cardstock using tape to make a washing line.

4. Now, from the same words you've used on the card stock, use the marker to write one letter on each clothespin. The clothespins will probably be too narrow to write the blended sounds together, but that's okay.

5. Challenge your child to use their fingers to attach the correct lettered clothespin in the correct order on each word card. Once they have attached all the letters, read the word aloud together.

Extension Ideas

Challenge your child to use the clothespins to make a whole new word of their choice, or spell out their name.

Learning

Children will learn to blend together the two sounds at the start of these words, which is a very important skill for reading. Use the words "pinch" and "squeeze" to describe the action needed to open the clothespin.

WORD BRACELETS

This activity looks at what we call split digraphs; that is, sounds that have a long vowel sound but have a consonant in the middle of the vowels. This is also sometimes referred to as "magic e," because when you have an e on the end of some words, it lengthens the first vowel sound. Examples include such words as sid + e = side, cub + e = cube, hop + e = hope and so on.

Supplies

Pen and paper

Letter beads

String or twine

How to

1. Write out a selection of the following words on a piece of paper for your child to see (or just ask your child to look in this book).

a–e	u–e	i–e	o–e
mane	cube	kite	hope
plane	dude	pine	robe
ate	cute	pipe	tote

First, read through the list of words together, sounding them out. Looking at the first three words, point out that the *a* sound changes when you add the *e* on the end.

2. Using your letter beads, choose a word and thread all the letters, except the final e, onto your string. Repeat the word, then slide on the e and ask your child to say the new word. Repeat for every word. When you're done, ask your child to choose their favorite word and they can wear the bracelet all day. Periodically, ask your child to read the word and when they feel confident with that one, exchange it for a new word.

Extension Ideas

When your child is ready, you can also include the *e-e* split digraph words—these may be a little longer than the other words. Examples include *Japanese*, *delete*, *concrete* and *these*.

Learning

In this activity, children learn that sounds can change if you add other letters to a word. It's worth noting that some split digraph words do not consist of an original word that changes to a new word when the e is added—for example, home. Some words—for example, *cut*, which becomes *cute*—also have a slightly different-sounding vowel sound than simply a longer vowel when the word changes. It's fine to discuss this with children if you feel they are ready.

PHONICS TRASH

This game is brilliant for children who love throwing! It combines hand-eye coordination skills with listening carefully to a sound and figuring out which digraph is in the word. Digraphs are written sounds that are made up of two letters, but only make one sound. For example, *ow* and *ou* are vowel digraphs that also happen to make the same sound. One of the most common issues that children have with spelling is choosing the correct digraph for their word, so emphasizing which they should choose for which word early on is no bad thing.

Supplies

2 small pieces of rectangular card

Marker

2 small trash cans or containers

Tape

Scrap paper

Extension Ideas

To make this a little trickier, the other person has to unscrunch and read the word aloud and then, without showing it, hand it to the other player to throw in the correct can. That way, they have to remember the correct spelling for the sound. You could even make it a real challenge by creating multiple trash cans for all the different digraphs (or just a selection) for a particular phoneme—for example, *ee* and *ea*, *e-e* and *ie*.

You can extend this idea for a whole heap of different sounds, too.

How to

1. Let's start by focusing on the digraphs *ow* and *ou*, but feel free to choose your own, based on what your child is working on or needs to work on. Write each of these digraphs on a piece of rectangular card and stick one on the front of each trash can with some tape.

2. Then, using other sheets of scrap paper, write out words for each digraph. Here is a list to help you:

shout, towel, cloud, cow, count, wow, mouth, how, about, flower

Other words you could use for more of a challenge:

loudest, mountain, sprout, proud, outside, howl, shower, downside, frown

3. When you've written them out, scrunch up the papers (kids will definitely like this part!) and put them in a pile.

4. Now you're ready to start! One at a time, take a scrunched-up ball, unroll it and read the word. Then, decide which can it should go in, scrunch it up again and throw it in! The person who gets the most words in the correct trash can wins the game!

Learning

In this game, children are learning to think about spelling as well as reading. By learning that one sound can have multiple different spellings, they are starting to think about reading beyond phonics. Fluent reading and writing can only be achieved when children start to understand that sometimes the way we say a word isn't necessarily the way we write it— or that there is more than one way to spell a certain sound.

POOL NOODLE WORD CREATION

Ever wondered what to do with all those leftover pool noodles that inevitably start to pile up in your garage? It's a surprising fact that there are actually lots of ways you can use pool noodles to help children learn to read. In this activity, we will be practicing the blends at the end of words.

Supplies

Craft knife or regular knife (adults only)

Pool noodle

Marker

Ruler or chopstick

Plastic box, for storage

How to

1. Carefully use a knife to slice your pool noodle into 1½-inch (4-cm) slices (do this part yourself). Keep three slices.

2. There are lots of ways you can use pool noodles for phonics, perhaps just focusing on the short words with a vowel in the middle (also known as CVC words), but if your child is ready, you can move on to words with blended endings.

3. Using your marker, write a series of letters around one noodle slice, for example the end blends *nk*, *nd*, *mp*, *st*, *ft* and *nt*.

4. Make sure that the letters you write on the other slices help complete words with those endings, such as *stink*, *hand*, *stamp*, *first*, *raft* and *ant*. Again, write at least three on each slice, ensuring the slices match up.

5. Now you're ready to begin! Slide each noodle slice onto your ruler or chopstick with the word endings first, followed by the corresponding slices. Then, ask your child to spin each slice around until they can make each word. Just remember that some words are shorter and others are longer, so there might be times when some of the slices aren't used. You will also be able to create some nonsense words, too. These are still important for reading as long as your child knows they aren't real words.

Extension Ideas

You can also write random letters on your pool noodle slices and encourage your child to make any words they like, sliding their pool noodle slices down a ruler, starting with their own name. If they need a little prompting, just refer to the word lists in this chapter.

Learning

By searching through the selection of pool noodle pieces, children will be totally immersed in the appearance of letters and finding the ones they need. This activity is also great for introducing word endings as well as the need to blend the letters together at the end of a word, rather than to say them as individual letter sounds. Great for improving reading speed!

PHONICS THEATER BOX

Children love making things out of cardboard boxes, and this activity is ideal for busy fingers!
Use craft sticks to make words, using some new sounds from Sets 8 and 9 (page 13).
Go through these new sounds first before starting this activity.

Supplies

Small box

Craft knife (adults only)

Around 20 craft sticks

Marker

Extension Ideas

Decorate your box so that it looks like a theater stage and encourage your child to use a silly voice to say the word, as if they are acting!

Learning

This activity gives children the chance to learn a new set of sounds in a very visual and memorable way. Using silly voices is also a great way of increasing the fun; and remember: more fun, more learning!

How to

1. Take your box and, using your craft knife, cut a series of lines at the top, just big enough for a craft stick to fit through (do this part yourself). On the end of your craft sticks, write a series of letters to make a selection of the words below. Write one phoneme per stick—for example, *squawk* would be split like this: *s-qu-aw-k*.

2. Possible words to use are:

jaw—j-aw	**cent**—ce-nt
draw—d-r-aw	**center**—ce-n-t-er
squawk—s-qu-awk	**circle**—c-ir-c-l-e
haul—h-au-l	**giraffe**—g-i-r-a-ff-e
maul—m-au-l	**general**—ge-n-er-a-l
wash—wa-sh	**judge**—j-u-dge
was—wa-s	**fudge**—f-u-dge
watch—wa-t-ch	**phonics**—ph-o-n-i-c-s
shawl—sh-awl	**alphabet**—a-l-ph-a-b-et
crawl—c-r-awl	**elephant**—e-l-e-ph-a-n-t
	chef—ch-e-f

3. Go through each sound with your child and then mix up all the craft sticks on your work surface.

4. Show your child the word list (you can either point to it in this book or write it down). Ask them to select the craft sticks that make a word on the list and to slot them into the top of the box, in order. Now, together, read the word aloud to see whether it makes sense. The sticks coming out of the top of the box will look like a little theater.

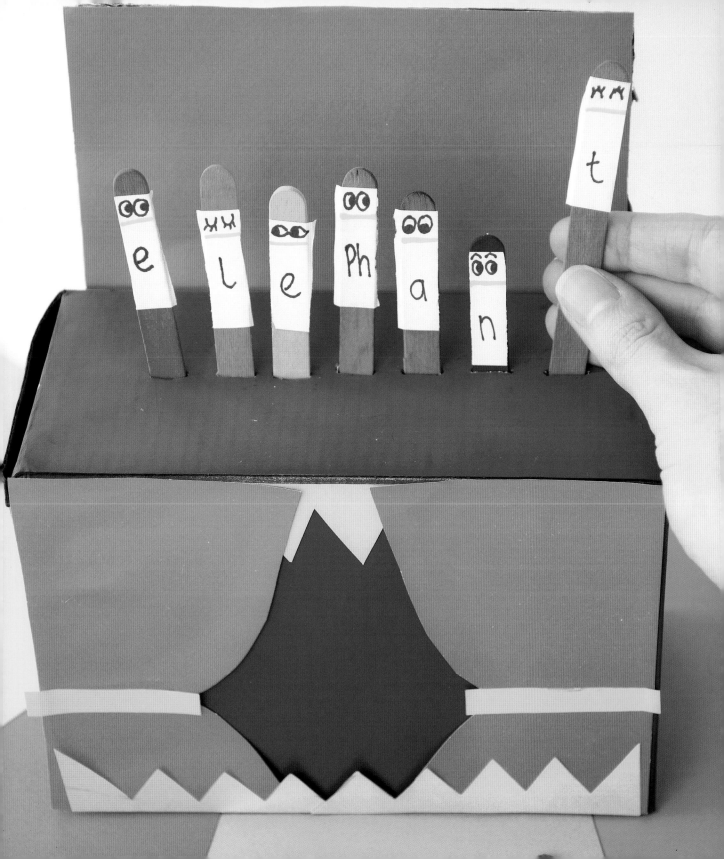

draw
was
moon

LETTER MAGNET WORD MAKING

Sometimes the older ideas really are the best, and making words from letter magnets has been popular with children ever since they were invented and put on refrigerators! This is a great little activity for children to play with when you're making dinner, and over time, gives them the opportunity to learn letter shapes and formations without even realizing it.

Supplies

Lower- and uppercase letter magnets

Magnetic surface, such as a fridge door

How to

1. Using the word lists from this chapter (or choose your own), spell out a selection of words on your fridge door or other magnetic surface, but leave out certain letters—leave out one letter if it's a short word, and two if it's a longer word.

2. Challenge your child to use the rest of the letters to complete the words on the fridge. If they're not sure, encourage them to try out a selection of letters until they think the word makes sense, then sound it out. There could also be more than one possible letter choice, of course!

Extension Ideas

To make this activity a little more challenging, try just putting one letter at the start of each word, including some of the capital letters. See whether your child can create their own word just by using the initial letter. For the capital letters, see whether they can figure out which kinds of words start with capitals—you might need to explain a little more about this.

Learning

By completing part of the missing word, children learn that you can often figure out a word even though you can't see, or don't know, every single letter, by using generalizations from the other words that they do know. This is important for children to understand, as it better allows them to sort and group their knowledge into manageable parts. This is a great activity to revise the sounds and words that children have learned in this chapter.

SIGHT
WORDS

Now it's time to move on to sight words, which are a list of words that occur frequently and need to be read automatically to quicken up reading speed. Sometimes sight words don't follow the phonic rules and so can't be decoded—for example, the word *said* (if you tried to sound this out, it would sound very different than the usual pronunciation—more like *s-ay-d*—as it doesn't follow the usual phonic rules). Some people call these "tricky words," or "common exception" words, but they all have one thing in common—they need to be learned by sight—hence the name!

In reality, when we become competent readers, all words need to be read by sight—even decodable ones—because we don't need to decode words anymore once we know them. Introducing sight words early on in your child's reading journey is important, as it helps them put sentences together, read books and generally make sense of the world more easily. It probably makes sense to work through this chapter in order. If your child finds the activities too easy, simply replace the suggested words with more complex words. Remember that you could also be dipping in and out of this chapter while working on the previous chapters, since sight words should be introduced at the same time as individual letter sounds.

Here is a list of sight words that your child needs to learn early in their reading journey.

a	is	are
and	it	her
away	jump	there
big	little	what
blue	be	Mrs.
can	you	could
come	they	see
down	were	the
find	was	three
for	oh	to
no	Mr.	two
he	asked	up
she	look	we
some	make	where
their	me	yellow
people	my	you
called	not	have
funny	one	like
go	play	so
help	red	do
here	run	when
I	said	looked
in	all	

SIGHT WORDS FLASHCARD RINGS

One of the easiest ways to learn sight words is through simple repetition and practice every day. Making sight words flashcard rings is easy and effective and can be used at any time—when you're waiting for swimming lessons to start, in a parking lot or before bedtime. Just whip out those flashcards and get practicing!

Supplies

Card stock

Scissors

Marker

Single-hole punch

Binder ring

How to

1. Using the list of sight words on page 97, create flashcards using your card stock, scissors and marker. Using your single-hole punch, punch a hole on the left-hand side of each flashcard. Open your binder ring and feed each card onto the ring, all facing the same direction, before you close it.

2. Go through each flashcard one at a time, reading it to your child and having them read it back to you. Start with just a few words each day, building up until your child can read the whole ring.

Extension Ideas

Once your child is comfortable with these words, pick out words from books that you think they need further work on, to add to the flashcard ring.

Learning

Although this isn't an especially creative activity, it allows for repetition of the sight words in an easy-to-store way and is a tried and tested way to learn sight words. Repetition is key here—the more they repeat, the more children will learn. Practice makes perfect, they say!

SIGHT WORDS PARKING LOT

What child doesn't love playing with cars? This sight word game combines the fun of parking cars with learning sight words, too. This creates an opportunity for child-led play where your child is doing incidental learning; you could call it "plearning"! All you need are your favorite toy cars, and you're ready to "plearn."

Supplies

Thick card stock—a large piece, if you have it

Thin card stock

Marker

Selection of small toy cars

Extension Ideas

Try writing the sight words on sticky labels and attach them to the tops of the toy cars. Then, without help, see whether your child can park the cars in the right spaces.

How to

1. With your child, create a parking lot from your card stock (you can use cardboard from packaging and boxes, too). Make your design as exciting as possible, with car spaces into which small toy cars could fit, crosswalks and a road. Select which sight words you'd like to work on and write them clearly in each of the parking spaces. Write the same words on smaller pieces of thin cardstock.

2. Show your child the words in the parking spaces and practice reading them together. Now, put your sight words, face down, in a pile and ask your child to pick up the top card. Read it out, then ask your child to park their car in the space that has the corresponding word. Keep going until all the spaces are filled.

Learning

Here, children get a chance to practice their sight words in a fun way that involves movement, fine motor skills and listening skills. Using their hand-eye coordination to guide the cars into the right position from one area of the game board to another, they will need to focus and use all their concentration skills to be the best car parker ever!

GUESSING GAME PHONICS

Remember Guess Who? What a great game it is! If you've got an old version of Guess Who lying around your house, now is the time to upcycle it and turn it into a fun game that children love! This game is terrific for keeping up with your child's level of learning—so you can keep reusing it forever!

Supplies

An old Guess Who? game

Card stock

Scissors

Marker

Extension Ideas

To make this game more challenging, you simply need to use more difficult words—try a mix of familiar and unfamiliar words, decodable and sight words to prompt conversations around new learning. If you don't have a Guess Who? board, you can always just use cards that you can turn over instead of flicking them down.

How to

1. Remove the cards that are already in the Guess Who? game box. Cut out pieces of cardstock that are the same size as the original cards and write some sight words on them, such as:

said, all, cat, dad, mom, we, ball, people, fit, hid, the, he, one, she, me, some, about

2. You can also include your own words or choose sight words from page 97. Then, put the new cards in the slots in the game board. You will need to do this for both Guess Who? boards.

3. Then, create slightly larger cards with exactly the same words on them. You only need one set of these.

4. Now it's time to set up your game. Each player should take a word from the pile of larger cards. The idea of the game is that each person has to guess their opponent's word by asking questions about it, and flipping down all the smaller word cards that don't correspond. For example, does it start with an *s*? Does it rhyme with something? Does it have more than three letters? For each question, you are only allowed to answer yes or no. For example, if the word has more than three letters, your opponent has to flick down every word on their board with more than three letters, until by process of elimination they have the answer.

Learning

This game gives children a chance to think about and examine the structure of words and to start to get a good grasp of words that cannot be decoded.

SIGHT WORDS TWISTER

Twister is a family favorite all around the world and never fails to make you laugh out loud. This game is great for coordination and balance, and to help learn rules and turn-taking. Use this fun game to help children learn new sight words—and move their bodies, too!

Supplies

Marker

Sticky labels

Twister game

How to

1. Write a selection of sight words onto white sticky labels. You will need two labels for each word.

2. Stick one set of sight words onto the circles on your Twister mat, and the others around the Twister spinner.

3. Now you're ready to play! Spin the spinner and, depending which sight word it lands on, ask your child to say the word and then move either their arms or legs onto that word on the Twister mat. Keep going for as long as you can!

Extension Ideas

Another way of playing this game is to use beanbags or something similar to throw onto the correct word when you spin it. Take turns so that your child gets to say some of the words, too, while you do the throwing.

Learning

Children always learn more when they are having fun; we all know that unintentional learning is way more effective than simple memorization tasks. And so children are more likely to remember the sight words if they have had to really look for them and move their body to get into the right position. This is great for problem-solving skills and general concentration, too!

CUP STACKER

Stacking cups is a pretty old-fashioned game, but sometimes the old ways are the best! In this game, your child will practice their sight words by building a tower with their cups. This helps build their motor and concentration skills wonderfully!

Supplies

Paper cups

Marker

Extension Ideas

For an extra challenge, ask your child to stack the cups in a way that they can make the words into a short sentence—the sillier the better!

How to

1. Choosing the sight words that your child needs to work on the most, write one on the side of each paper cup, one word per cup.

2. Taking turns, see who can build the highest tower with the cups, reading each word as you put the cup on the tower. If the tower falls down, you have to start again! See what kinds of towers you can build, how high, how wide. How many cups does your child predict they can use before the tower falls down? Work some math into it, too!

Learning

This activity is all about the repetition of sight words, but making it fun at the same time. The more children are exposed to the sight words, the more quickly they will learn them and the quicker they will progress in their reading journey.

MYSTERY WORD PAINTING

Everyone loves a mystery, and this activity combines pretending to be a spy with sight words—a sure-fire winner! Using crayons and paint to uncover each mystery word, your child will be hungry to figure out each word, which means that they will learn unintentionally—perfect!

Supplies

White crayon

White paper

Water-based paint

Paintbrush

Water-based felt-tip pens (optional)

How to

1. Using the list of sight words on page 97 at the start of this chapter (e.g., where, yellow, you, have, like, so, do, when, looked) or your own choice of words, use the white crayon to write the words on your white paper (or use any color crayon with the same color of paper). Make sure you remember where you've written them and to space them out, too, or it might become a bit of a jumble!

2. When you're ready, tell your child there are some mystery words written on the paper and it's their job to find them, using the paint and paintbrush. Watch your child as they uncover each word and then encourage them to read the word out loud, helping them if need be. If you don't have paints, water-based felt-tip pens will work just as well!

Extension Ideas

Now your child might like to try writing the mystery words themselves! Let them do so, encouraging them to space out the words so they don't overlap, then you do the painting—if they'll let you!

Learning

This activity is a great way to not only practice sight words but to also talk about why the paint doesn't coat the crayon. Science mixed with reading!

SIGHT WORDS MAGIC SHOW

Children are naturally inquisitive and love "magic," even when it's to do with reading! Take advantage of their natural curiosity with this fun hide-and-seek game that will have them reading without even knowing it—you can also use the paper cups from a previous activity in this book.

Supplies

3 paper cups

Marker

Small object, such as a mini figure

How to

1. Using the sight word list on page 97 at the start of this chapter, write out a selection of sight words on at least three paper cups. If the words are becoming too easy, or your child already knows them, here are some additional words you could use:

had, an, back, as, at, get, if, him, into, his, of, got, off, on, but, will, that, this, then, them, with, now, too, went, it's, from, children, just, don't, old, I'm, by, time, house, about, your, day, made, came, saw, very, put

Extension Ideas

Try this game with ten or more cups so that your child has to read more words to get to the fun object. Don't forget to keep mixing them all up every time!

2. Placing the paper cups in a row, secretly conceal the small object under one of the cups, then mix them around like you sometimes see in magic shows. Together with your child, read the words on the cups. Now, it's time to play! Ask your child to say the word on each cup and to lift it up to see whether the fun object is underneath. Keep going until the object has been found, then swap places so that your child gets a chance to be the "magician."

Learning

This activity gives children a chance to practice and repeat the sight words in a very motivating and fun way, since they will be really eager to find the hidden object. When children have fun, they remember more!

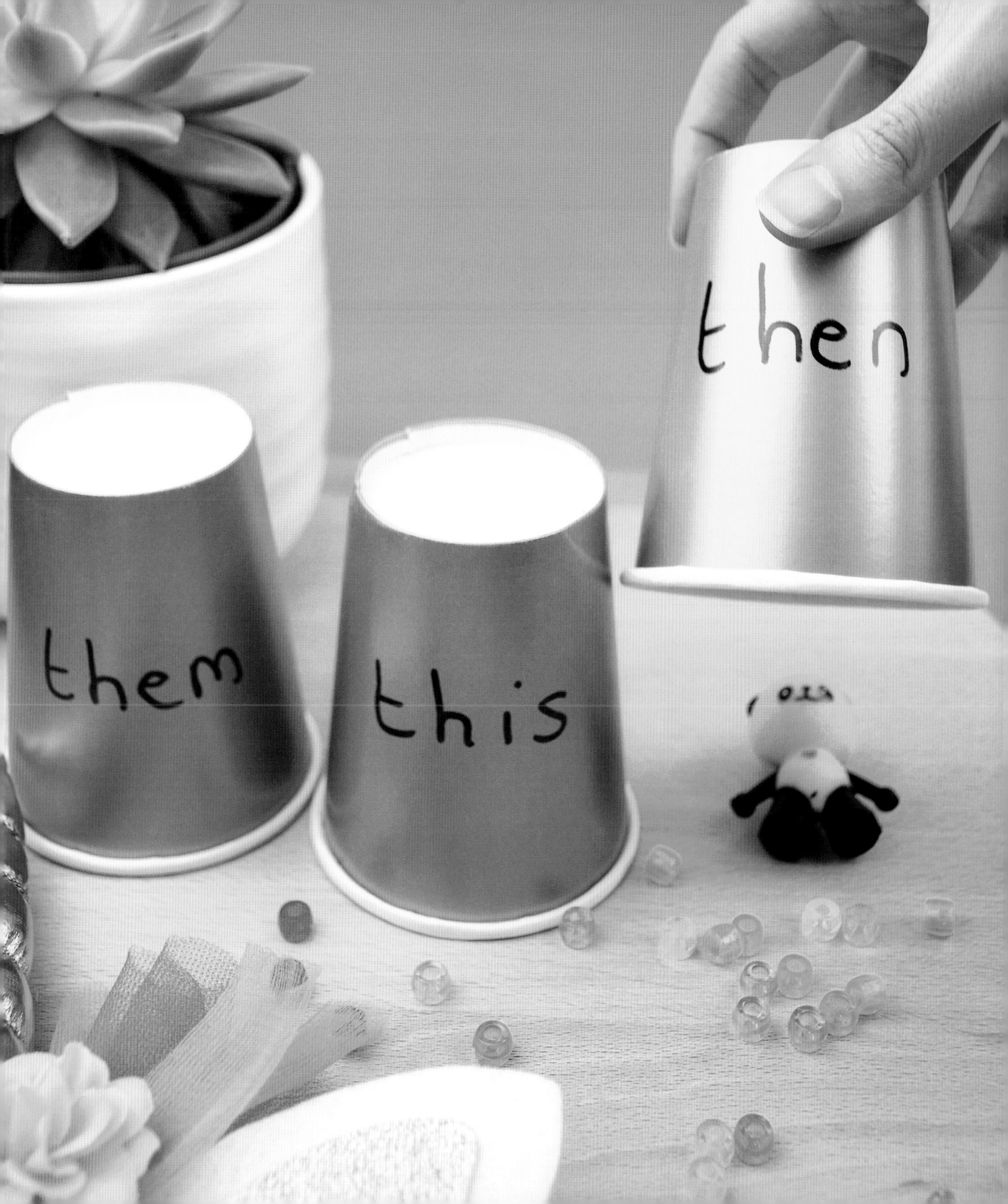
then
them
this

SIGHT WORDS BOWLING

Bowling is a fun and active way for children to practice sight words and learn a new skill, too. This game works really well both indoors and outdoors, and is great for hand-eye coordination, fine motor skills and turn-taking.

Supplies

Sticky labels

Marker

6 bowling pins, wooden if you have them

Small ball

How to

1. Using either the sight words in this chapter (page 97) or other words your child is working on, make sight word labels and stick them onto each bowling pin. Ask your child to help set up the bowling pins in the usual triangular formation, then you're ready to start!

2. Encourage your child to roll the ball toward the bowling pins, then ask your child to read out all the words on the pins they have knocked over, before setting them up again and having another turn. Another way to play is to try to be really skillful and target a specific word to knock down before rolling the ball. Don't forget to take turns!

Extension Ideas

Combine reading and writing! After each turn, ask your child to write down the sight words they've knocked over, to keep score. See who wins!

Learning

This game provides a great opportunity to practice sight words and fine motor skills at the same time, as getting those pins to stand up and balance can be quite tricky and requires careful attention. Writing down the sight words to keep score works really well for memorization, too.

GIANT BUBBLE WRAP SIGHT GAME

Ever wondered what to do with leftover packaging? This fun sight word game gives children the chance to practice their sight words while bouncing around—something that is bound to go over well—and it also makes great use of something that is otherwise of no use to you.

Supplies

Marker

Large Bubble Wrap

Extension Ideas

To extend this activity, simply use a selection of increasingly difficult words to challenge and introduce new sight words to your child's vocabulary. If they're ready, see whether your child can jump from word to word in a way that makes a sentence, even (or especially) if it's a silly one.

How to

1. Using your marker, and on each large bubble, write one sight word from the list on page 97 at the start of this chapter. Either indoors or outdoors, lay out the wrap, words side up, on the floor or ground.

2. As you say each word, ask your child to jump to that part of the Bubble Wrap. Make the distances between words bigger as they jump from word to word, to make it a little trickier. Now change places and have your child read out the words while you do the jumping!

Learning

Seeking out each word before jumping and making a big popping sound is a sure way to help children retain information and consolidate sight words they already know. The more memorable and fun an activity is, the more likely children will want to take part—and remember what they did!

BEANBAG MATCHUP

This game is great for outdoor playtime and can be used just about anywhere! Throwing beanbags is such a great way to practice throwing and catching skills. They are much easier to handle than balls, and a useful way to work on hand-eye coordination, too. Add the reading element and you've got a recipe for learning!

Supplies

Chalk

3 beanbags

How to

1. In your yard or other outdoor area, choose sight words (either using the ones from page 97, or other words your child is working on), use your chalk to write them on the pavement and draw a ring around each one. Write them quite large so they are clearly visible from a few yards away. Then, draw a line that shows clearly where your child should stand.

2. Time to start! Take your beanbags and ask your child to throw them onto each word, one at a time, calling out the word before they throw the beanbag. Another way to play is to take turns calling out the words for each other. Or you can just throw a beanbag randomly and see where it lands, reading out the closest word.

Extension Ideas

Try throwing the beanbag over your shoulder for an additional challenge, so you can't see where it's going, then read out the word nearest to where it lands. So much fun!

Learning

Concentrating on throwing the beanbag and thinking about which word it is going to land on is great for practicing and repeating sight words. Repetition is key here, but don't be afraid to introduce new words, too.

SIGHT WORDS SNAP

Use craft sticks to make a fun snap game, perfect for a rainy day! Snap is an easy-to-learn-and-explain game with no complicated rules, and also teaches children the skills of anticipation and turn-taking.

Supplies

20 craft sticks

Marker

Container, such as a cup or pencil holder

How to

1. Choose some sight words, either from page 97 or from the words your child is currently working on, and write them onto craft sticks, making sure that you write the words right at the end of the craft stick and that there are two sticks for each word.

2. Now, place your craft sticks in the container, word end down, so they can't be seen. Taking turns, take out one craft stick, place it on a flat surface and read it out loud. The other player should select and then lay their craft stick on top. If it's the same word, whoever shouts "Snap!" first gets to keep both sticks. Keep going until you've used up all the sticks. Whoever gets the most sticks wins the game.

Extension Ideas

You could also turn this into a memory game by laying down the sticks on a flat surface with the word side facing down. Taking turns, turn over each stick, say the word, then try to find the matching stick. Keep the sticks in the same position, to try to remember where each one is. Whoever matches the sticks gets to keep them. Continue until all the sticks are matched.

Learning

Matching the words correctly takes quite a lot of concentration and attention to detail. This means more learning as children will naturally look at the word closely, which will help them remember it.

MIRROR WORDS

Children are naturally interested in anything mysterious or out of the ordinary, and this mirror word activity is perfect for anyone who is struggling to get their child to focus on the sight words they have to learn. All you need is good backward-writing skills!

Supplies

Small hand mirror

Pen

Card stock or paper

Extension Ideas

If your child feels ready, see whether they will try writing the words backward with you while using the hand mirror. This will require quite a lot of concentration and fine motor skills practice, but something that they will find fascinating!

How to

1. This activity works best if you prepare it while your child is occupied with something else, as it can take a few minutes to get right. Hold the mirror in the best position to allow you to write out the sight words backward on the card stock. This might take a little bit of time and practice, but don't rush—take your time. You can use the sight words from page 97 in this chapter for this activity.

2. When you're done, it's time to call your child over. Say that you've accidentally written the words backward and need their help to understand them, using the hand mirror. Show them how to hold the mirror in position to read out the words one at a time. You'll be amazed at how excited they'll be to figure out each word.

Learning

Children love uncovering mysteries and figuring things out. This activity will alert them to the fact that the letters have to be in a certain order and formation to make sense. Using the mirror will give them an "Oh!" moment as they realize what each word is. Something they will remember!

SIGHT WORDS BAKING

Baking is a fun kinesthetic activity that brings people together, so why not use it for practicing sight words and make something yummy at the same time? Here, you can choose to actually bake something, or use playdough instead. If you do decide to bake, gingerbread dough works really well.

Supplies

Gingerbread dough or playdough

Rolling pin

Letter-shaped cutters

Baking sheet

How to

1. Looking at the sight words on page 97, choose a few that you know your child needs more work on.

2. Choose one of the words and, rolling out your dough, say the word to your child and see whether they can spell it. If they can't, simply write it down for them to refer to. Ask them to use the letter-shaped cutters to cut out each letter, one at a time. Then, lay the cutouts on the baking sheet. If you do choose to use gingerbread dough (which, let's face it, is more fun), you can now bake them according to the recipe or package directions. Once they're cooled, ask your child to read the word again, and then they can eat the gingerbread!

Extension Ideas

Using the gingerbread dough, you could also cut out other shapes and ice them with the sight words you're working on. Your child can eat the shapes once they've read the word (maybe space this out a bit so they're not eating lots at a time!).

Learning

Making the letters of a sight word your children find a little tricky is a great way to consolidate learning, as you're factoring in the smell and feel of the letters and the look of the whole word. Adding the taste of the gingerbread just makes things more fun and memorable!

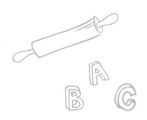

2A

2B

2C

2D

SIGHT WORDS MATCHUP

This game is a really fun way for children to understand the component part of sight words. This is also a game that children are very familiar with and so should require little explanation and preparation time, especially if your child is a little impatient!

Supplies

Pen

Paper

Scissors

How to

1. Choose which sight words you'd like to focus on, either from pages 97 or 110 or other words your child is working on. Write out each word, in quite large letters, on a whole piece of paper.

2. Cut out the letters into squares. Then, in smaller letters at the top of each square, write the whole word.

3. Now, spread out the squares on a flat surface. Ask your child to match up the letters to form their corresponding word. Then, read the word aloud. Repeat for all the words.

Extension Ideas

You could try this game without the word written on each square, to see which words your child can make from the letters all on their own.

Learning

Searching for the letters to put together to make a word and referring to the whole word on each square will allow children to learn new sight words really easily while having fun! It also serves as a useful reminder that sight words are made up of parts and may follow spelling rules that children already know.

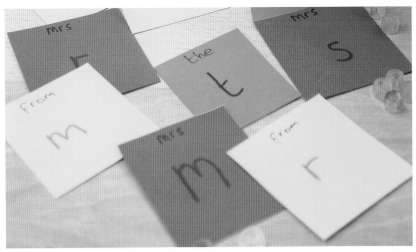

SIGHT WORDS JIGSAW PUZZLE

Get those fingers moving! For this activity, you can use an old jigsaw puzzle that you don't need anymore, by turning the pieces upside down, or buy a blank jigsaw puzzle from a dollar store or similar source. The key is giving your child the opportunity to think about the spelling of sight words, as well as the reading, as it all fits together perfectly. Just as jigsaw puzzles do!

Supplies

Blank jigsaw puzzle

Marker

Extension Ideas

Create another jigsaw but this time, write one word on each jigsaw piece to make a sentence. See whether your child can put them in the right order.

How to

1. Identify which sight words you'd like to work on today, using words from pages 97 or 110, words that your child finds more challenging from this book or totally new words. Using your marker, write one letter per word on adjoining pieces of the jigsaw puzzle, so the whole word joins up across the pieces. Continue to write other words on the pieces until you have used up all your jigsaw pieces.

2. Separate all the pieces and jumble them up.

3. Now ask your child to start putting the pieces together, reading the letters and words as they go. When each piece is used up, the jigsaw puzzle is finished!

Learning

With this activity, children will start to think about the spelling of sight words as well as reading them. This is a really useful skill for reading and writing, and will help with the retention of words.

MEMORY GAME

Memory games are ideal for improving the focus, concentration and thinking skills of children of all ages, and this fun game is a low-preparation way of encouraging children to remember their sight words.

Supplies

Large sheet of paper

Marker

Package of sticky notes

Extension Ideas

Try this game using up to 40 sight words, to add an extra element of challenge.

How to

1. On your large sheet of paper, sketch out a rough grid, making sure that each grid square is large enough to write a word in—about the size of a sticky note. Try to aim for at least 20 squares on your grid. Choose which sight words to focus on, either from pages 97 or 110, or from other words your child is working on. Write your sight words on your grid, but make sure you write two of each word, each in a separate grid space. When you're done, cover each word with a sticky note and it's time to get started!

2. Taking turns, ask your child to uncover two words at a time, reading them aloud; then, you take your turn. When a player uncovers two matching words, then they can keep those two sticky notes. Keep going until all the words are uncovered. The person with the most sticky notes wins!

Learning

Memory games are great for enhancing cognitive skills and encouraging speaking and listening. The added motivation of trying to remember what word is in each position works wonders for remembering that word for future use.

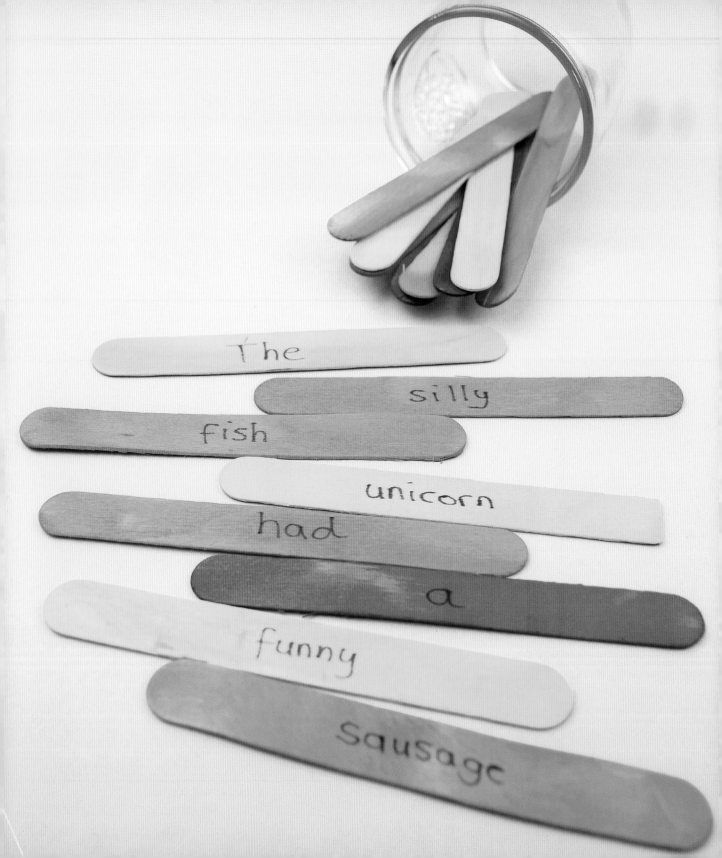

SENTENCE READING

Congratulations! You made it through the phonics activities and sight word practice, and now you're ready to make sentences with your child—the key to effective reading. In fact, you can use this chapter anytime to start encouraging your child to use the words they know in sentences; there's no need to wait until you've covered all the previous activities. Even if they only know a few letter sounds and words, these activities will still work just fine.

In this chapter, your child will have the chance to learn how to properly construct sentences using knowledge they already have, but didn't know they had. Learning in this way is great for confidence. Add the engaging and creative activities we have planned, and your child will associate fun with learning and reading. Just what it takes to be a world class learner! You can choose to either follow these activities in order, or zip around in any order you please.

BOTTLE CAP SENTENCES

This game is great for outdoor and indoor learning. If you don't have bottle caps, simply use pieces of cardstock or paper instead.

Supplies

Around 10 milk bottle caps (washed first)

Marker

How to

1. Think of a sentence, or ask your child to do so—for example, "Gran said it was a fun day for a picnic" or "The cat is fat." Write each word on a bottle cap and then scatter them around a room or an outdoor area.

2. Now, say to your child that you're going to make a sentence together. Call out each word, one at a time, and ask them to hunt for the cap with that word and bring it back. When they've retrieved all the words, say the sentence again and ask your child to put the words in the right order, then read them together.

Extension Ideas

A nice way to extend this activity is to do the same thing but this time with a "silly sentence," maybe even one that doesn't make sense. Ask your child to suggest the silly sentence, and then ways that it could be changed so it makes more sense to a reader.

Learning

In this game, children will use their attention and reading skills to seek out words, read them and then put them in a sentence in the right order. They will learn that sentences are made up of individual words and that these words need to be placed in a particular order. Try clapping out the syllables in the words for the whole sentence, to help them start to feel the rhythm of things.

SILLY SENTENCE CRAFT STICKS

Making sentences—especially silly ones—using craft sticks is huge fun and also very versatile, as there are so many ways you can use them. A whole heap of sentences can be made just by moving the sticks around and there's no sense of "I made a mistake," as the sillier the sentence, the better! Use a combination of sight words, decodable words and pronouns—such as *he, it, we* and *she*—just to make things more interesting!

Supplies

Marker

About 30 craft sticks

Container, such as a cup or pencil holder

How to

1. Write a series of words (whatever your child is working on) on your craft sticks, including some pronouns, some sight words, animal names and anything else that you think would interest your child—for example, *he, it, we, she, the, my, unicorn, was, silly, flowery, like, a, rainbow, sausage, funny, fish, yellow, said, mom, went.* Include some short words as well as longer, more challenging words.

2. Place the craft sticks in your container and then ask your child to pick out about six sticks and read each one aloud. Place them on a flat surface and then ask your child whether they can make a super silly sentence from them. The sentence doesn't have to make sense, but be prepared to talk about why it doesn't, and which words can be inserted to improve it. Put all the sticks back, then choose ten sticks. Carry on until you've made at least five sentences.

Extension Ideas

When you've used up all your sticks, spread all of them out and use them to make the silliest sentence you can together! Look at the words again and start to identify the verbs and nouns in the sentence. Explain that verbs are doing words and that nouns are objects or things. If it's helpful, you can even color code the words!

Learning

During this activity, children will start to think about sentence structure and what makes a good—or silly—sentence. You can start to draw attention to the concept of verbs and nouns at this stage, as this will be helpful to children in the future when they think about how to correctly form a sentence, but only if they're ready.

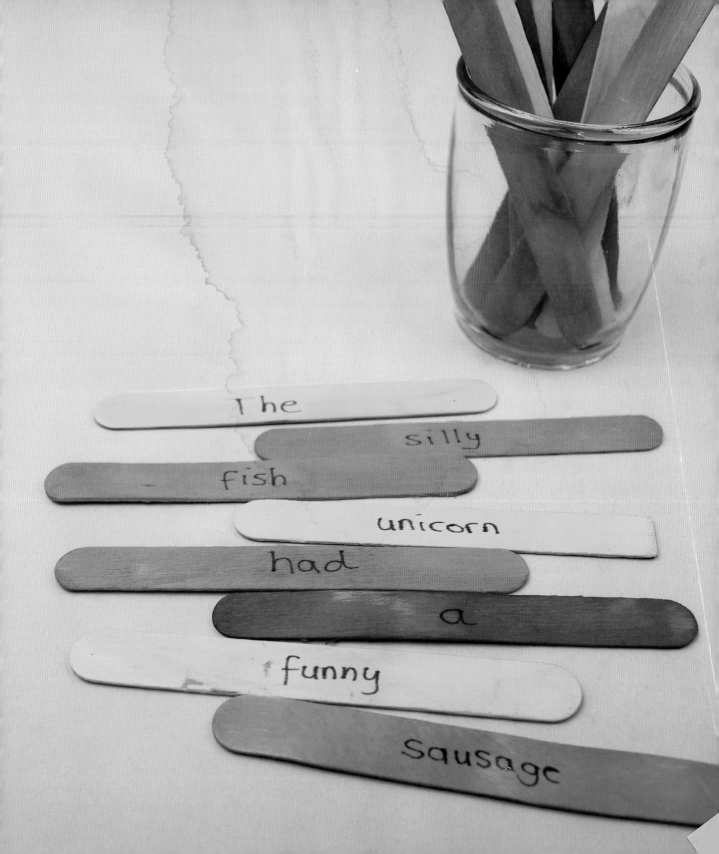

SENTENCE BUILDING BLOCKS

Making sentences using building blocks is not only superexciting, but also great for both fine and gross motor skills, too. Children learn so much better when they're engaged with play, and what better way to learn to make sentences than with building blocks that are so much fun to begin with?

Supplies

Sticky labels

Marker

Selection of large building blocks of different sizes

Extension Ideas

If your child is ready, encourage them to try to create a silly story using the words, creating sentences that connect together. Read the story together and discuss what could happen next.

How to

1. On your sticky labels, write a selection of words, including some of the sight words your child has learned. Make sure you include some pronouns, such as *he*, *she*, *it*, *they* and *we*. (You can also include adjectives, such as *big*, *small*, *loud*, *good*, *happy*, *scary*, *smelly*—whatever you think would work well for your child.) Stick each note to the side of a block. When you're done, scatter the blocks around and ask your child to stack them, build them—whatever they prefer—so that the words make a sentence.

2. If your child is more preoccupied with building at this stage, don't worry; they will soon notice the words and ask you about them. When your child has made a few sentences, read them out together to see whether they make sense. Encourage your child to be really adventurous in their word choice—or suggest new words for you to add.

Learning

Making sentences that connect together is a key reading—and writing—skill. Children will start to think about the meaning behind the words rather than just the words themselves.

COOTIE CATCHER SENTENCES

Cootie catchers are so much fun, and this activity is perfect for revisiting sight words and putting them in a sentence together with decodable words. Remember: the sillier, the better! Including words your child is interested in—such as *unicorn, pirate, soccer, dancing* or *trains*—will also increase their motivation.

Supplies

Sheet of blank paper

Scissors

Pen or pencil

How to

1. First, fold your paper to make a square, cutting away the excess. Now, fold in all four corners, turning your paper over when you're done, then repeat. Next, turn over again and fold all the corners into the center one last time. With this cootie catcher, you need to write on it when it's already folded, as this makes it easier to figure out what to write where.

2. It's important for this activity that you write the words in order, so that the sentences have some hope of making sense. This activity works best by writing out questions, as it makes it so much more fun. On the outer section of your cootie catcher, write a question as a short phrase—for example, *can a, how will, does a, does my* or simply *my* or *your*.

3. On the next section, write eight subjects for your sentence—for example, *dog, cat, boy, girl*. On the next layer, write four verbs—for example, *eat, like, love, drive*. On the inside section, write four different words to complete the sentence—for example, *fast, snails, sausages* or *milkshake*. Make up your own selected terms and see how silly you can be! Don't forget the question mark at the end.

4. Now you're ready to start! Simply use the cootie catcher to read a range of silly sentences, taking turns. So fun!

Extension Ideas

You can extend this activity by choosing more challenging words and making the sentences longer and sillier!

Learning

Cootie catchers are a fun way of generating lots of different sentences very easily, and encouraging children to think of their own words, too. Great for vocabulary building.

ROLL A SENTENCE

This is another wonderful game for sentence creation, using dice! This works best if you have some dice already at home, or you can make one by marking numbers 1 through 6 on a cube-shaped object. Either way, it's very entertaining!

Supplies

Paper

Pen or pencil

6-sided die

Whiteboard and dry-wipe pen

How to

1. For this activity, you need to have a series of words listed in six columns on a piece of paper, one for each number on the die. You can choose whichever words you like, or use ours here:

> **1**—that, the, her, she, his, him, we
>
> **2**—house, place, idea, sky, sea
>
> **3**—is, a, of, it, in, on, under, an
>
> **4**—empty, fun, sad, dirty, clean
>
> **5**—rabbit, horse, fairy, unicorn, doctor
>
> **6**—huge, tiny, funny, furry, smelly, rainbow

2. Ask your child to roll the die and choose a word from the list according to which number the die lands on. Write the word on your whiteboard. Continue to throw the die and write the word that comes up until you have about ten words to choose from.

3. Now, together, choose some of those words to make a sentence. Point out to your child that they need different types of words so that a sentence reads correctly and makes sense. Write it out on the board, then read the sentence aloud to your child—does it need extra words to make sense? Which ones?

4. Make as many sentences as you like by again throwing the die, then read through the sentences together to see which is your favorite.

Extension Ideas

Instead of reading the sentence together, challenge your child to try it on their own!

Learning

In this activity, children learn that there are lots of different ways to create sentences, and this is a great skill for both reading and writing. This activity is also useful for introducing new vocabulary and discussing the meaning of new words as well as for talking about word types and why we need them.

SENTENCE BUILDER CARD GAME

By now, your child should be getting used to the idea that there are different types of words and without them, sentences often don't make sense. In this activity, children will learn to construct sentences using these types of words. It also introduces the concept of plural words.

Supplies

Different colored cards

Scissors

Marker

4 containers, such as cups or pencil holders

How to

1. Cut your card into strips in order to make cards of individual words from the following lists, or make up your own lists. Be sure to keep the same list words together in one container.

> **List 1**—boys, girls, babies, cows, buffalos, aliens, monsters, fairies
>
> **List 2**—love, take, dance, walk, talk, eat, play, jump
>
> **List 3**—kind, disgusting, smelly, stinky, old, interesting, awful, lovely
>
> **List 4**—ladies, flowers, milk, mud, grass, spaceships, woodland

It might be easier to write words from the same list onto the same color card so they don't get mixed up.

2. Now it's time to start! Ask your child to take one card from each container, then use the words to create their own sentences by putting the cards in order. Remember you might need to change the endings of the words so that the sentences make sense. When you've created the sentences, read them all together. Remember, as always, the sillier the better!

Extension Ideas

Keeping your sentences in order, change one word from the sentence by replacing it with another word card. Does it still make sense?

Learning

In this activity, children will increase their understanding of sentence structure. Understanding sentence structure is really useful as a reading skill, as it helps us make sense of the meaning of sentences and put them together to gain a wider understanding of the book or text we are reading. It's also valuable for learning other languages.

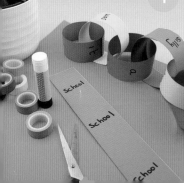

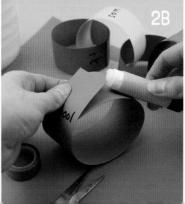

SENTENCE PAPER CHAINS

Making paper chains is great for celebrations, such as birthdays and Christmas, and there's no need to buy them when you can make them so easily at home! For this activity, use a birthday as an excuse to make some fun sentence paper chains, or just make them anytime!

Supplies

Different colored thin card stock

Scissors

Felt-tip pen

Sticky tape or glue

How to

1. Cut your card stock into long, thin strips. Write a selection of words on the strips, one per strip, using words either from this book, words you know are related to your child's interests or words that your child is learning or needs to work on. Show the words to your child and read through them together, clapping the syllables of each word.

2. Now ask your child to take some of the word strips and put them in order to make a fun sentence (you may need to add some connecting words so the sentence makes sense!), connecting the strips together as a paper chain, and using your sticky tape or glue to secure the strips. When you're done, read the sentence together on your chain. Continue until all the word strips are used up. Put up the chains and keep reading them back throughout the day for extra practice. Clapping the syllables each time you read is fun, too!

Extension Ideas

Another way of using paper chains is for you to start a sentence and for your child to suggest the ending themselves, writing them out independently on the chains. Try to get them to use as many interesting words as possible!

Learning

This activity is a great way for children to see how words connect together to make sentences in a meaningful way. If you use a word your children are unfamiliar with, it's useful to teach them to read around the word to try to figure out the meaning and pronunciation of the word they're having trouble with. It's good to also tell children that they don't necessarily have to understand every single word if they can understand the gist of something, though it's useful for vocabulary building to look back later and find out the word's meaning, either in a dictionary or by asking an adult.

SCRAMBLED SENTENCES

By now your child will probably be getting a firm grip on reading in sentences, so for this last activity, I wanted to do something really fun to get their creative juices flowing!

Supplies

Sticky notes

Pen

How to

1. Write the words for a series of objects on your sticky notes, one per note—household objects are great for this. Go around the house putting them in random places, then ask your child to go around finding, reading and collecting the sticky notes.

2. While they're doing that, write out some more sticky notes with such words as *the, it, is* and a series of adjectives, such as *horrible, lovely, awful, tiny, huge* (try to make them as funny as possible!) and then various names of people you know or who are in your family.

3. When your child is ready, show them the new sticky notes and see whether they can use them, together with the sticky notes from the household objects, to create a funny story. When they're done, go through the sticky notes together, reading what they've created, and moving the sticky notes around to make things even funnier!

Extension Ideas

Collect all the sticky notes and replace them with words that are new to your child. Can they make a new sentence with the unfamiliar words?

Learning

Using the sticky notes in this way allows children to experiment with lots of different words in a familiar setting and to understand that having words in different positions in a sentence can make a huge difference to the meaning of that sentence, too. It also shows them that they only need to know a relatively small number of words to be able to read a large number of sentences—great for confidence building!

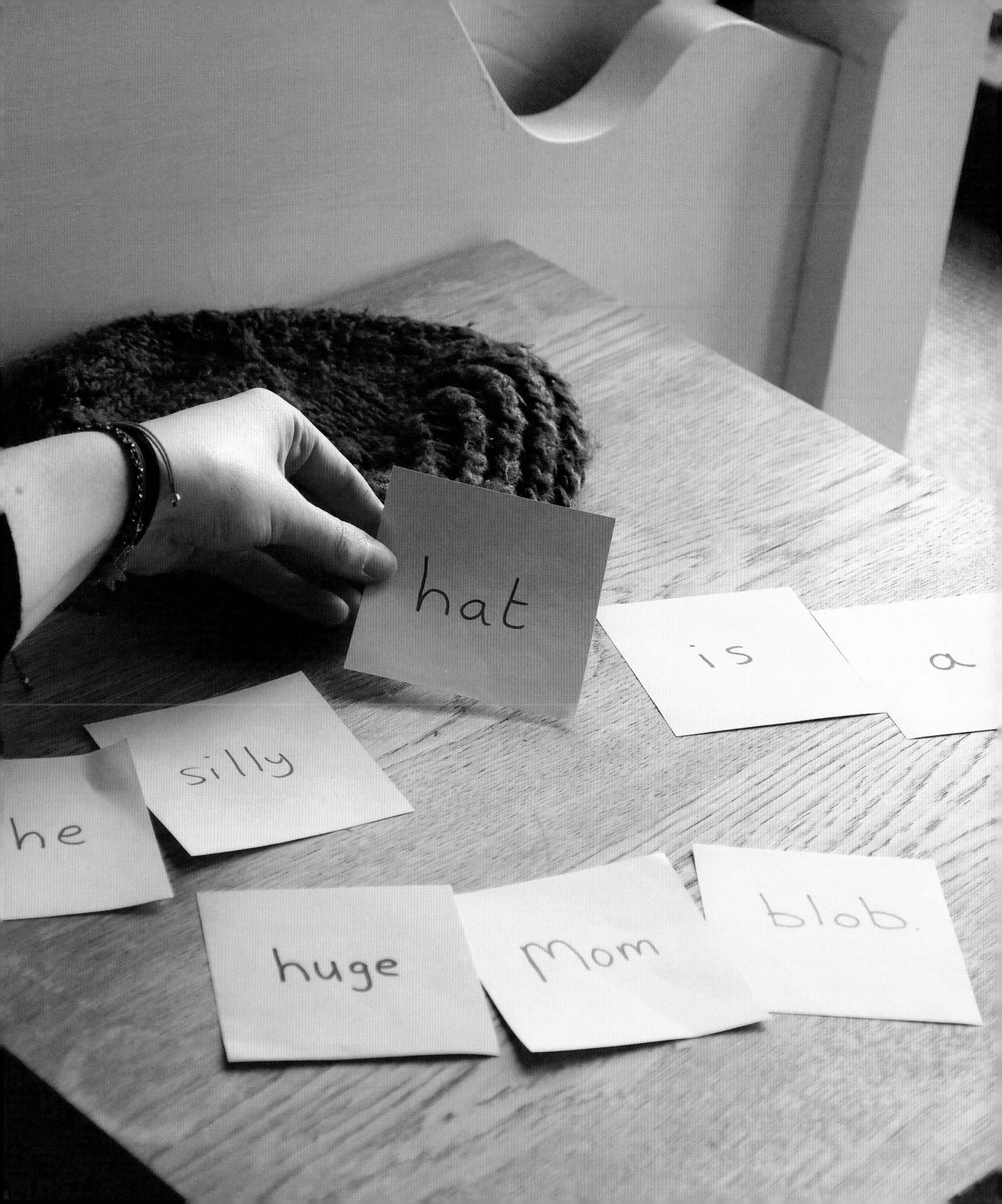
hat
is
a
silly
he
huge
Mom
blob.

REVIEW

How did you do? Reference my phoneme list section at the start of the book (pages 12–13) to check each phoneme and see whether there are any gaps in your child's knowledge. Then, review the sight word lists on pages 97 and 110. If there are gaps, simply go over those sounds with a different activity.

Most of the activities in this book can be adapted for different sounds and words, so you can cover the phonemes in lots of different ways.

Reading is everything, and by enjoying the activities in this book with your child, you are giving them an important gift: the ability to associate reading with pleasure.

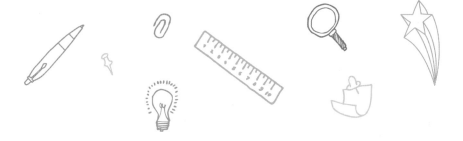

ACKNOWLEDGMENTS

There are a few very important people in my life without whom this book could never have happened. First of all, my good friend Maggy Woodley, for inspiring me, encouraging me and being an amazing sounding board. To Emma Vanstone, for your wisdom, cheering me on and for generally being a legend.

Then there are the people in the Mrs Mactivity family—Sophie Pickles, for being my sense checker, all-around Early Years expert and go-to person for pretty much everything educational, as well as being a lovely person. Hayley Price, for your friendship, creative genius, artistic ideas, amazing photography skills and being great with my kids. Without you there literally would be no Mrs Mactivity. And then, to our Mrs Mactivity community—your support for what we do makes me smile every single day.

To the crew at Page Street Publishing, for believing in me, giving me a chance and guiding me through this whole process. I thank you.

A shout out to the Swan Avenue community, for providing me with skittles, egg boxes, bottle caps and more!

And lastly, my family: My husband, for putting up with all the late-night research and prop creation and for going out to work every day so I can follow my dreams. I hope to do the same for you one day. My children, for agreeing to be in the photographs, advising, helping and inspiring me. To my parents, for their support, belief in me and limitless help with childcare and fixing things around the house. Thank you for everything.

ABOUT THE AUTHOR

Heather McAvan is a qualified teacher with over ten years' experience in the classroom and sixteen years within education. She has taught all over the world, including Japan, Spain and Yorkshire, England, and has taught a range of ages from four to eighteen. Heather is also the founder of the creative learning website Mrs Mactivity—and leads the team that creates exciting hands-on printable activities for teachers and parents to make learning fun for kids.

Heather is also a mom of three children who inspire, criticize, encourage and generally make all her hard work worthwhile. In her spare time, Heather likes spending time with the family rabbit, Jeff.

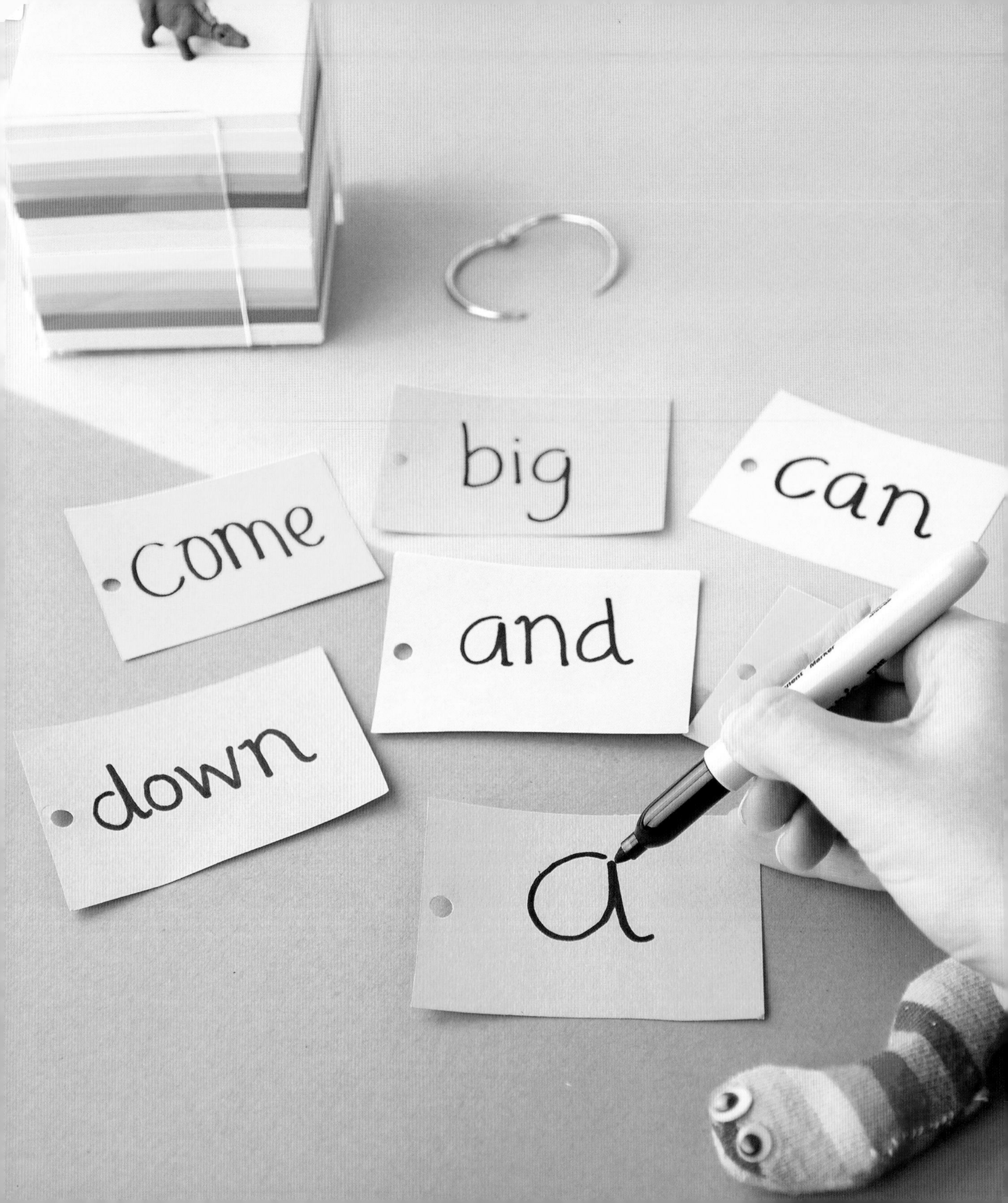
big
can
come
and
down
a

INDEX

DISCARD